2-1-2025

Lieutenant Colonel George A. Larson, USAF (Ret).

THE 54TH
FIGHTER-INTERCEPTOR SQUADRON

4880 Lower Valley Road • Atglen, PA 19310

Other Schiffer Books by the Author:
Thunder Over Dakota, ISBN: 978-0-7643-4263-9
Great Plains Warriors of World War II, ISBN: 978-0-7643-4379-7
The History of Dyess Air Force Base, ISBN: 978-0-7643-4822-8

Copyright © 2017 by George A. Larson

Library of Congress Control Number: 2016958433

All rights reserved. No part of this work may be reproduced or used in any form or by any means—graphic, electronic, or mechanical, including photocopying or information storage and retrieval systems—without written permission from the publisher.

The scanning, uploading, and distribution of this book or any part thereof via the Internet or via any other means without the permission of the publisher is illegal and punishable by law. Please purchase only authorized editions and do not participate in or encourage the electronic piracy of copyrighted materials. "Schiffer," "Schiffer Publishing, Ltd. & Design," and the "Design of pen and inkwell" are registered trademarks of Schiffer Publishing, Ltd.

Type set in Zurich BdEx BT/Times

ISBN: 978-0-7643-5239-3
Printed in China

Published by Schiffer Publishing, Ltd.
4880 Lower Valley Road
Atglen, PA 19310
Phone: (610) 593-1777; Fax: (610) 593-2002
E-mail: Info@schifferbooks.com

For our complete selection of fine books on this and related subjects, please visit our website at www.schifferbooks.com. You may also write for a free catalog.

This book may be purchased from the publisher. Please try your bookstore first.

We are always looking for people to write books on new and related subjects. If you have an idea for a book, please contact us at proposals@schifferbooks.com.

Schiffer Publishing's titles are available at special discounts for bulk purchases for sales promotions or premiums. Special editions, including personalized covers, corporate imprints, and excerpts can be created in large quantities for special needs. For more information, contact the publisher.

I dedicate this book to the members of the 54th FIS who protected the skies of the north central United States, along with those of the Nike Surface to Air Missile sites, Rushmore Air Force Station, and Ellsworth Air Force Base.

CONTENTS

Preface 6
Introduction 8

History of the 54th FIS

Nike Surface to Air Missile Defense of Ellsworth Air Force Base 11
54th FIS Training 26
54th FIS 33
Crash of F-86D 34
54th FIS 54
Live Airborne Test of Air-to-Air Missile Armed with Nuclear Warhead 55
Northrop F-89J 56
Nuclear Weapons Storage (WSA) Area on Ellsworth Air Force Base 62
54th FIS 62
54th FIS Awards 69
Advanced Training 70
Functions of 54th FIS 64
54th FIS (1959) 89
Winning the Hughes Trophy 92
Air Defense Terms 103
54th FIS 107
54th FIS Training Annex 109
Sundance Air Force Station (Radar Warming Site) 116
Atomic Energy Commission (AEC) Power Plant at Sundance AFS 118
Deactivation 121
Epilogue 124

Appendices 126
Glossary 168
Notes 169
Sources 179

PREFACE

During the height of the Cold War between the United States and the Soviet Union, each nation felt threatened by the other's nuclear weapons. The United States started to develop and expand its air defense capabilities to knock down Russian Air Force long-range, heavy, strategic nuclear bombers flying from Russian northern Arctic staging bases, over the North Pole, across Canada, and into the northern United States to drop nuclear free-fall bombs on US military targets and major cities. Air Defense Command created a vast network of air command centers, radar stations, ground observer corps, and fighter-interceptor squadrons. One of these squadrons was the 54th Fighter-Interceptor Squadron (54th FIS), based at

Ellsworth AFB, east of Rapid City, South Dakota. The squadron protected the Strategic Air Command's assets at Ellsworth AFB, including nuclear bombers, tankers, and intercontinental ballistic missiles. From 1951–1960, the men of the 54th FIS protected North America from possible air attack by long-range Russian Air Force bombers. The threat was deemed real at the time, and only later shown to be less serious as the CIA overflew the Soviet Union with high-flying Lockheed U-2 reconnaissance aircraft. These flights ended on 1 May 1960, when the Russians shot down a U-2 piloted by Francis Gary Powers. Regardless, the dedication of the men who maintained 24-hour watch on American skies is outstanding. When I completed my book *History of Ellsworth Air Force Base, 1941–2011*, former members of the 54th FIS started calling and dropping off information and photographs on their unit, asking me to do a book on their fighter unit. Most of this material was previously determined nonexistent.

INTRODUCTION

The 54th Fighter Squadron (modern) is an inactive USAF air combat unit. The squadron's last active/operational assignment was to the 3rd Operations Group, Elmendorf AFB, Alaska, flying F-15C/D Eagles, which was inactivated on April 28, 2000. The squadron's early history started in WWII, when it was activated on January 15, 1941, at Hamilton Field, California. The 54th Fighter-Interceptor Squadron became an important Cold War player in the protection of Ellsworth AFB, South Dakota. The squadron operated at Ellsworth AFB December 1, 1952–December 25, 1960. The squadron flew three different types of turbojet powered fighters to protect Air Defense Command (ADC) defense sectors for the United States. The Republic F-84 Thunderjet proved to be the most successful fighter-bomber during the Korean War (1950–1953), although outclassed by the Russian Air Force MiG-15; it had limited air defense capability. Its replacement, the North American F-86D Sabre Dog, was armed with unguided air-to-air rockets. When the squadron upgraded to F-89J Scorpions their lethality increased, with the aircraft carrying atomic-tipped warheads and early conventional high-explosive air-to-air missiles. The Strategic Air Command (SAC) wanted to protect its bomber bases (including Ellsworth AFB) from attacking Russian Air Force long-range bombers carrying gravity atomic bombs, as well as its planned Titan I Intercontinental Ballistic Missile (ICBM) sites in South Dakota near Ellsworth. Air Defense Command added surface-to-air Nike missiles for another layer of close-in (point) air defense: first, the conventionally armed Nike-Ajax, followed by the Nike-Hercules capable of being armed with

Introduction

Hardened Underground Bunkers

conventional or atomic warheads. Because of the large nuclear weapons storage area at Ellsworth, the 54th FIS had assembly, storage, and maintenance facilities for its nuclear weapons. This also applied to one Nike Hercules site at Ellsworth. The fear of a Russian nuclear attack on the United States nearly came to a head during the Cuban Missile Crisis. The belief was it was not if there would be a nuclear war (WWIII) with the Soviet Union, but when!

Because the mission of the 54th FIS involved nuclear weapons, even in 2015, the majority of its official Air Force unit records were classified (secret and confidential); though declassified in November 1978, they still required a request to be released (marked unclassified). Some unclassified files were recovered from a former administrative clerk assigned to the squadron; when the unit was removed from Ellsworth, these records were saved and provide a look at the early history of this squadron, its aircraft development, and its mission.[1]

The 54th FIS has a proud military history (lineage). The squadron matured as it transitioned from piston fighter aircraft to early turbojets, to supersonic interceptors armed with sophisticated air-to-air missiles. This transition of aircraft development follows the history of the squadron and its importance to the defense of the United States from WWII to the war on terror. The 54th FIS' story provides a look at the transition from piston-engine fighter aircraft to turbojet all-weather fighter-interceptors.

HISTORY OF THE 54TH FIS

History of the 54th FIS

1941

The 54th FIS was activated at Hamilton Field on 15 January 1941.

1941–1942, the squadron flew the Curtiss P-36.
1941–1942, the squadron flew the Curtiss P-40 Warhawk.
1941–1942, the squadron flew the Republic P-43 Lancer.[1]

1942

22 January 1942: The squadron moved to Paine Field, Washington. Flying conducted in P-40s and P-36s.
13 February: The First P-38 arrived.
9 March: Designation of the squadron changed from the 54th Pursuit Squadron (Interceptor) to the 54th Pursuit Squadron (Interceptor) AAF.
2 April: First accident: Lt. Morse was injured when his P-38 crashed into the mess hall, killing two airmen.
5 April: Lt. Pinson crashed into Puget Sound—killed.
9 April: Reconnaissance mission to Elmendorf, returned on 22 April; the first step toward combat.
12 April: Designation changed from Pursuit to 54th Fighter Squadron AAF.
23 May: 1st Air Echelon (pilots and mechanics) left for Elmendorf and arrived 2 June, then to Cold Bay and Umnak.
24 May: 2nd Echelon to Elmendorf, arrived 2 June.
25 May: Departure of the rest of the squadron to Kodiak via sea transport by 29 May.
31 May: Arrival at Elmendorf.
3 June: Initial tactical operation of 54th was an air alert; two hour patrol, no bandits.
4 June: First planned mission (escort), no contact with enemy.
5 June: First air echelon left for Cold Bay, 2nd flight to Fort Glen, Umnak.
6 June: Search mission for enemy carriers, no success from Cold Bay. First active strike from Fort Glenn, Umnak. Strafed a Russian freighter flying Japanese colors.
14–15 June: A and B Flights left Elmendorf for Fort Randall, Cold Bay, Alaska.
18 June: Capt. Jackson (CO) promoted to major.
21 June: Lt. Millton was killed in a crash; weather was the cause.
5 July: C-53 crash, four officers killed.
21 July: Lt. Stoland—fourth in a flight of four—was killed in a crash into a mountain in bad weather.
21–23 July: Second part of air echelon departed Fort Glen, Umnak, and arrived at Adak Island on 31 August.
3 September: Squadron began attacking the enemy on Kiska. Lts. Walter and Laven strafed and bombed.

11 September: Squadron was switched to the 342nd Fighter Group from the 55th Fighter Group.
11–19 September: Third part of the air echelon arrived at Adak-PCS.
13 September: Lts. McCoy and Hsenfus contacted Zeros, the latter badly shot up. McCoy damaged one Zero.
14 September: Lts. Mills, Gardner, and Laven get one Zero a piece. Maj. Jackson (CO) was killed in an air collision with Lt. Crowe (also killed). 1st Lt. Victor E. Walton was CO for six days.
20 September: Maj. Ashkin from the 11th Fighter Squadron assumed command.
23 September: First tactical operation against Amchitka Island: bombed a radio shack and sunk a submarine.
3 October: Lts. Walton and McDonald get two more Zeros.
7 October: Lts. Long and Ambrose get air medals, first decoration.
14 October: 2nd Lt. Luther B. Stockard shot down, died in a water bailout.
18 October: 1st Lts. Walton and Laven received DCS.
27–31 October: Capt. Francis Pope named the new CO.
9 November: First attack on Attu, eight killed by strafing.
28 November: 1st Lt. Kenneth Ambrose killed in a crash returning a P-38 to the United States.
17 December: 1st Lt. Richard B. Gardner earned the first Purple Heart.
26 December: Capt. Matthews killed in combat.
30 December: Lts. Kaiper and Leighton were lost.

1943

The squadron flew the Lockheed F-5 (P-38G) photo-reconnaissance aircraft.

9 January: Capt. Morgan A. Griffin named the new CO.
13 February: A Mitsubishi Type 97 was downed by Capt. Griffin and Lt. Moore. Capt. Laven and Lt. Evans each got a Zero.
March: Replacement 1st Lts. Long and Hasenfus were the first to go home.
12 March: Four C-47s and ten P-38s left Adak for Amchitka airstrip.
2 April: Capt. Harley Taulkes succeeded Maj. Griffin as CO.
30 April: The remainder of the squadron arrived at Amchitka from Adak.
May 4–6: Pre-invasion bombing and strafing of Attu (the 54th played a large role in each). An early attempt at close air ground support by fighters.
26 May: More victories. Lt. Col. Wattl got one Betty, but was later lost on a mission. Lt. Moore got three Bettys. Lt. Higgins, one Betty.
4 June: Concluded operations against Attu Island.
11 June: Attacks against Kiska Island. Lt. G. B. Martin was killed in weather.
18 July: Capt. William T. Samways assumed command of the 54th.
July: Ten missions over Kiska, no aerial combat.
14 August: Last tactical mission flown against Kiska.
15 August: Invasion of Kiska by Canadian and American troops.

30 September: Second part of air echelon TDY to 344th Fighter Squadron to participate in practice flights with bombers.
18 October: Squadron ordered to Shemya-PCS. At this time detachments from the squadron were at Shemya and Attu.
October: Bad living conditions and only training; low morale.
November: Official change of station for the entire 54th to Alexai Point, Attu Island.
November–December: Digging in and setting up on Attu Island.
25 December: Christmas turkey and trimmings on Attu Island.

Awards Received by 54th
(January 15, 1941, to December 31, 1943)

Distinguished Service Cross	2
Silver Star	2
Distinguished Flying Cross	33
OLC to DFC	4
Air Medal	38
OLC to Air Medal	11
Purple Heart	3

Losses of the 54th (January 15, 1941–December 31, 1943)

Tactical Officers Killed	9
Wounded	6
Non-tactical Officers Killed	10
Enlisted Killed	7

Accomplishments

59 enemy aircraft destroyed and damaged
10 vessels damaged

1944

15 January: Third anniversary party of the squadron.
27 January: Lt. Banks killed in weather during a routine search mission.
4 February: Lts. Garver and Dailey killed in mid-air collision.
May: Opening of Pilots Rehabilitation Center; training flights continued.
June: Completion of the Day Room, "Pride of the Aleutians."
6 June: D-Day in Europe.
July: Routine training—first rotation.
August: Two original sergeants—Sgts. Stevens and Price—killed in an auto crash due to bad weather; routine training.
September: Routine training. "Rags" the mascot killed by a truck.
October: Squadron acquireds cow named Saide from the Navy, the only cow on the Aleutians; routine training.

The 54th Fighter-Interceptor Squadron

November: Twenty-one pilots arrived, eleven left.

24 November: The Rehabilitation Center burnt down.

December: Rotation of 37 enlisted men, 36 new ones arrived. Fifteen new pilots relieved nine old ones.

3 December: Three pilots killed: two in a mid-air collision, and one who bailed out in the water after engine fire. Rash of accidents: six majors destroyed four planes and two minors attributed to low pilot flying time.

25 December: Christmas party.

1945

15 January: Fourth anniversary. Squadron won a pool table tournament.

14 February: Six new P-38Ls arrived.

13 April: First sighting of Japanese balloons. Six shot down.[2]

The 54th was assigned to combat air patrols (CAPs) with its P-38Ls from Alexai Point Army Airfield, Attu, Alaska Territory, November 20, 1943–March 8, 1946. It was in an ideal location for high-altitude performance aircraft to intercept and shoot down Japanese high-altitude, long-range incendiary carrying unmanned balloons.

In early 1944, the Japanese Army and Navy consolidated their long distance armed balloon programs. The army's balloon (Type-A) was constructed of paper from the Kozo bush, with 600 separate sections glued together. The navy's balloon (Type-B) was made of rubber. The balloon weapon program was named Operation *Fu-Go*. The balloon bomb launches were a historically significant event in the development of an advanced concept at the time: waging intercontinental warfare from one's own country to that of an enemy. The first balloon launch was initiated on the birthday of former Japanese ruler Emperor Meiji, November 3, 1944, at 5 a.m., as strong eastward jet stream winds shifted direction toward North America. The jet stream is a narrow band of high velocity winds near the base of the stratosphere where the tropopause makes its greatest change in elevation. During the winter months, jet stream winds can reach a maximum of 450 mph, with the average lower across the Pacific, along the Aleutian Islands, Alaska, and Pacific coast into North America. Launch sites were built along the lower half of Honshu Island, east and northeast of the Tokyo plain.

Nakoso (6 launch pads)
Otsu (9 launch pads)
Ichinomiya (6 launch pads)

The primary balloon design was simple and functional: 32.8 feet in diameter with a capacity for 19,000 cubic feet of hydrogen, constructed of four-ply paper upper surfaces and three-ply paper lower surfaces. Launching these balloons was a complicated process. The balloon was carefully positioned on a ground launch pad to a suspension curtain attached to the mid-seam and secured with three-foot-long ground screw anchors. The balloon was inflated with hydrogen from gas cylinders until volume reached 50%. This allowed the balloon's volume to increase as it climbed to maximum altitude. A wooden suspension cradle held the balloon's aluminum equipment ring with altitude control equipment, sand bags, and bombs. As the inflated balloon stretched in its moorings ground crew personnel allowed the balloon to rise; with the 49-foot shroud lines fully extended it lifted the ordnance package off the ground and the balloon was released to climb into the jet stream for the high-altitude flight to North America. The Japanese could not have begun its balloon bombing attack at a more favorable time. First, the November jet stream was strong, shoving the balloons rapidly toward North America. Second, the American public had just been informed of the German V-2 rocket attacks against England, along with hints of the possible development of long-range rockets that might be able to hit cites along the East Coast. This was more speculation than fact, but still bred a lot of doubt. Third, American deaths from kamikaze attacks were increasing and revealed the extent the Japanese, already being bombed by B-29s based in the Mariana Islands, were sacrificing their own airmen to defend against approaching American task groups. Fourth, a successful balloon bombing attack against the United States would be a morale builder for Japanese civilians suffering because of US submarine sinkings of food, fuel, and strategic material transports from the Greater Eastern Asia Cooperative Sphere (countries under Japanese occupation), and the bombing of Japanese cities by US Navy carrier battle groups and B-29s (including the disastrous incendiary raids burning cities to the ground, displacing hundreds of thousands of Japanese).

Once each balloon launched, a timer powered by a one and one-half volt wet cell battery determined when the bombs released. This was one technical error by the Japanese that prevented most of the bombs releasing. At altitudes above 10,000 feet, the wet cell batteries could freeze, preventing the bombs' release. If the Japanese used dry cell batteries many more bombs might have been released, causing the level of damage originally anticipated. The balloon's length of flight was programmed over a specific time, determined by estimating the jet stream's eastward velocity. The balloon was equipped with aneroids to maintain a height of approximately 30,000 feet and remain centered in the jet stream. The aneroids carried on board each balloon consisted of a disk-shaped metallic vacuum to measure changes in air pressure to maintain altitude. If the balloon dropped below its planned altitude, the aneroids sensed the altitude decrease, triggering the release of sand bags to allow a climb back to maximum altitude. If the balloon reached a higher than planned altitude the aneroids opened the gas relief valve at the bottom of the hydrogen gas bag, bringing the balloon down to the desired altitude. The release of expanding hydrogen inside the gas bag was necessary to prevent the balloon from climbing to a height where increased pressure would burst the thin paper covering, bringing it down to the water or ground. The balloon was still at the mercy of jet stream winds determining the outward route from Japan to the United States and Canada.

The Japanese launched the following number of balloons against the United States:

Date	Balloons to be Launched	Balloons Actually Launched
November 1944	500	700
December 1944	3,500	1,200
January 1945	4,500	2,000
February 1945	4,500	2,500
March 1945	2,500	2,500
April 1945	0	400
Total	15,000	9,300

A very conservative estimate is that only 10% of the launched balloons actually reached Canada and the United States because the wet cells froze and did not allow altitude to be properly achieved. A high percentage of balloons recovered in the United States retained their bombs for the same reason, providing the US intelligence on the bomb release mechanism. The onboard flash bomb on each balloon ignited one hour twenty-two minutes after the last bomb release, allowing many balloons to be recovered intact. The balloons were usually armed with one fifteen kilogram high-explosive bomb or one twelve kilogram incendiary bomb and four one kilogram incendiary bombs.

Recovered balloons usually indicated some of the ballast and cargo detached when hitting the ground or water. Army examination and investigation of these balloons revealed that the sequence of ballast release stopped before the payload released, so the bombs were not armed. The bombs had to be released from the carrying platform to arm.

The balloons were intended to start forest fires in the American northwest, possibly destroying cities and war industries in the path of the fires.

The first discovery of a Japanese balloon bomb was on November 4, 1944, when the crew of a US Navy destroyer patrolling 66 miles southwest of San Diego, California, recovered a deflated balloon with rigging and mechanical apparatus on a metal ring. Naval intelligence officers determined the equipment was designed for indiscriminate bombing of the United States from the Japanese home islands. Warnings were sent to Army Air Force bases along the most probable inbound route of the jet stream along the coast from Alaska to Washington. The difficulty locating airborne balloons was shown the evening of November 4, when four 4th Air Force Curtis P-40 Warhawks based at Los Angles AAFB scrambled to intercept an unidentified object over Santa Monica. The P-40 was not a night fighter, and none of those launched intercepted the suspected Japanese balloon. The first confirmed shoot down did not occur until February 23, 1945, when a Lockheed P-38 Lightning intercepted a Japanese balloon over Calistoga, California. The first confirmed Japanese balloon bomb explosion in the United States occurred on December 6, 1944, fifteen miles northwest of Thermopolis, Wyoming. AAF personnel recovered metal fragments from a fifteen kilogram anti-personnel bomb. On January 4, 1945, two men working in a field near Medford, Oregon, heard a loud explosion and saw a spurt of flames twenty to thirty feet high, followed by a cloud of yellow smoke in a nearby field. When they arrived at the scene, they found a hole in the ground about six inches in diameter and twelve inches deep. The sides of the hole appeared baked. Further investigation revealed a burned cylindrical metal casing and pieces of molten metal, indicating the object was very likely an incendiary bomb. A hook identical to those used on the shroud lines of the balloons was also found.[3]

The record of how many (partial number from one 54th FIS monthly report) Japanese balloons 54th pilots shot down is not available, but balloons were intercepted and shot down, preventing them from reaching the American northwest and farther into the western states.

May: V-E Day.
11 May: Lt. Wilson killed, engine failure on take-off. Al Jenkins and troop (USO) arrived—big party, with girls.
25 July: CO Lt. Col. Samways TDY to C&GS School, not expected to return. CO July 18, 1943–July 25, 1945. Maj. Andis assumed command.
14 August: V-J Day.
August: Many inspections by generals; 54th does quite well. Considered an example to other squadrons in the area.
9 October: Maj. Harrison assumed command.
26 October: Squadron left Alexai Point for Anchorage.
1 December: Lt. Bickett relieved Maj. Harrision as CO.

1946

1942–1946, the 54th FIS flew the Lockheed P-38 Lightning.

January: Lt. Preble relieved Lt. Bickett as CO.
15 January: Fifth anniversary party.
21 March: The 54th Fighter Squadron was deactivated.

The squadron was inactive until December 1, 1952. When reactivated, it was mainly built about a nucleus of personnel from the 175th Air National Guard Squadron of South Dakota. Following is the summary September 1946–December 1, 1952, for the 54th Fighter-Interceptor Squadron.

September: 175th ANG Squadron formed at Sioux Falls, South Dakota. The squadron was previously carried on records as 387th Fighter Squadron. Lt. Col. Joe Foss was the first 175th CO.

1948

Summer camp held in Sioux Falls.

1949

Summer camp at Casper, Wyoming. During the year, the 175th received the Spaatz Trophy for the best squadron in the ANG. The F-51 acrobatic team was made up of Lt. Col. Foss, Lt. (at that time Capt.) W. J. Downy, Lt. J. Beyer, and Lt. R. Reid.

1950

Summer camp at Camp Williams, Sparta, Wisconsin. Maj. D. L. Corning was promoted to lieutenant colonel and made CO.

1951

18 January: Squadron alerted for activation in March.
1 March: Squadron went on full-time active duty without ceremonies.
17 May: Squadron went on alert status.
14 June: Lt. P. J. Kirkby killed in crash in an F-51, lost control in pattern.
27 June: Maj. Gen. R. R. Acheson of CG of CADF informed squadron of a move to Rapid City AFB in the near future.
19 July: Lt. Helder, with Capt. W. Swenson in the back seat, ground looped the squadron's T-6 ($1,400 in damages).
16 August: Squadron completed move to Rapid City, now equipped with F-51s.
September: Alert hangar completed and F-51s moved in.
15 November: Lt. K. D. Frank killed after complete engine failure during a gunnery mission.

1952

1952–1953, the squadron flew the North American F-51 Mustang.

21 January: Fire destroyed squadron supply building, $4,000 in damages.
January: The 175th won a $100 Base Ground Safety Award, also the leadership trophy. Winds up to 100 mph and temperatures below zero held down flying.
March: Twenty-one squadron pilots participated in gunnery exercises at Yuma, Arizona. Twenty pilots rated expert.
May: Flying virtually halted because of nationwide gasoline strike.

August: Permanent alert hangar completed and F-51s moved in; much more comfortable for pilots and crew chiefs.
15 September: Lt. J. D. Brown bellied in from GCA pattern with a dry fuselage tank.
27 November: Lt. V. G. Howe landed gear up at Sioux Falls, pilot error.
1 December: 54th Fighter-Interceptor Squadron reactivated, takes over from the 175th. New CO is Lt. Col. Paul J. Imig.
18 December: Squadron received word that turbojets were forthcoming to the 54th—morale boost.
28 December: Lt. Norris brought in the first flight of three F-84Gs. Existing aircraft used on alert until replaced by the F-86D, all-weather interceptor in January 1954.

1953

1953–1954, the squadron flew the Republic F-84 Thundersteak.

16 February: Squadron transferred from 31st Air Division (AD) to the 29th AD. During the month heavy snow held flying to a minimum.
16 March: First gunnery mission in the F-84.
23 March: First night flying in the F-84.
31 March: F-84s assumed alert duties.
24 May: Fifteen aircraft and 22 pilots departed for gunnery at Yuma, Arizona.
5 June: Lt. Harre bailed out after an explosion and fire returning from a gunnery mission, first squadron ejection.
10 June: Lt. E.M. Koski killed in a crash, inclement weather.
24 June: Capt. Cobb killed in the crash of an F-84, cause unknown.
18 September: Lt. Col. W. P. Benedict relieved Lt. Col. Imig as CO.
November: The squadron began making preparations for change over to the F-86D in the near future. Many pilots TDY to "Dog School." Technical representatives for several companies conducted F-86D maintenance courses.[4]

1954

Arrival of the F-86D
The *Rapid City Journal* reported the first F-86Ds arriving at Ellsworth AFB:

"The calm cold of Ellsworth AFB was shattered by an ear-splitting roar Friday morning as the first of 26 of the nation's newest all-weather defense fighters arrived at the local bomber base. Piloted by Lt. Col. William Benedict, Squadron Commander of the 54th Fighter-Interceptor Squadron, was a gleaming, new F-86D, sister ship to the Sabre jet, which became famous as a MiG killer in the Korean War. Lt. Col.

Benedict, after performing several smooth maneuvers over the long Ellsworth AFB runway, brought the high-speed North American jet to a perfect landing and parked it near the 54th ready hangars on the southeast corner of the base. He was greeted by squadron officers and civilians representing firms that constructed the fighter. The new fighter, which was flown from Southern California, will replace the Republic F-84 Thunderjets flown by the squadron.

"Lt. Col. Benedict: 'It [F-86D] will increase the air defenses of Ellsworth many times. The F-86D is equipped for all-weather flying and once held the world's speed record. Rapid City home and business owners won't have to worry about the reverberating 'boom' from planes breaking the sonic barrier.'

"Built by North American Aviation, the Sabre (F-86D) is similar to the fighter used during the Korean War, except for added electronic equipment and rocket tubes, and has reached a maximum speed of 715.697 mph, which is faster than the speed of sound. The total elapsed time for Lt. Col. Benedict to fly from Los Angeles, California, to Rapid City, South Dakota, was two hours. He made the first lap to Ogden, Utah, in one hour and ten minutes, then flew from Ogden to Ellsworth AFB in 50 minutes.

"Lt. Col. Benedict: 'Could have made it faster too. I was flying at less than 100 percent of power and didn't have the afterburner in operation.'

"The 54th is an ADC fighter unit assigned to Ellsworth for protection against sudden attack. It maintains an around-the-clock alert plan where pilots can get into the air within two minutes. After landing, Lt. Col. Benedict: 'She's a beautiful ship to fly but hard to get used to. On take-off at Los Angeles, I got a porpoise motion [The aircraft follows an undulatory flight path about a median line of flight, often the result of short-period longitudinal oscillations.] and the same thing happened at Ogden, Utah, during landing. This was because the fighter's controls are extremely sensitive. The F-86D has power steering and power brakes. It is just like driving a new Buick. On the F-84, it takes two hands to pull out of a dive. On this ship, you just barely pull back with your thumb and forefinger.'

"Lt. Col. Benedict, a veteran Air Force pilot, has logged 5,000 hours flying time, including 1,000 hours in turbojet aircraft. He has 15 hours in the F-86D. When the fighter taxied to a stop curls of smoke from the brakes rose into the air.

"Lt. Col. Benedict: 'I'm not used to those power brakes. It takes about three times as much push in the Thunderjet. The Sabre jet, on numerous occasions, has broken windows when it passed through the sound barrier. However, this will be averted in Rapid City as the squadron plans to carry out its tests in a sparsely populated area.'[18]

"The first of 26 F-86Ds to be assigned to the 54th FIS was piloted to the base this past week by Lt. Col. William Benedict, 54th Commander. Flying indirectly from the factory in Los Angeles, Lt. Col. Benedict arrived with the new aircraft in two hours. The F-86Ds will replace the outdated F-84s now assigned to the station. However, the F-84s will stay here until complete transition to the new plane is made.

"The F-86D is an all-weather version of the famed MiG killer, the Sabre jet. It is a lone striker and the best all-weather interceptor the Air Force has. The new fighter has over five miles of electrical equipment in its body, enough electronic devices to build a television station, and weighs approximately 10 tons. It fires rockets. Although the F-86D is capable of breaking the sound barrier, it is known as a 'trans-sonic' plane and not a supersonic jet.

"Lt. Col. Benedict: 'We won't be breaking any windows around here. When an aircraft goes through the sound barrier, it sounds like a charge of TNT and windows break. The F-86D broke the standing speed record some years back with a speed of 715.6 mph. This was later broken by a British aircraft. The Navy brought the title back to America and the Air Force's F-100 took the world record from the sailors. The squadron would be checked out in the interceptor as fast as they [ADC] give us hours.'

"At present, the 54th FIS leads all ADC squadrons in the United States for flying hours and combat readiness. Along with the F-86D come Mr. J. D. Moore and a four-man instruction team from North American Aircraft Company and specialists from Hughes, Lear, Philco, and General Electric Companies to instruct and teach the pilots and men of the 54th FIS the fundamentals of the aircraft."[5]

A 54th FIS F-86D at Ellsworth AFB.
Courtesy South Dakota Air and Space Museum archives

1954–1957, the squadron flew the North American F- 86D "Dog" Sabre jet.

January: Two dozen more F-86Ds arrived shortly thereafter. F-84s continue on alert until about half the pilots were checked out in the "Dog." All personnel were on a seven-day work week to speed checkout in the "D."
22 January: Col. Benedict brought in the first F-86D.[6]

The *Rapid City Journal* had additional reporting on the arrival of F-86Ds for the 54th FIS:

"The change-over from Thunderjets to Sabres will take about a week officers pointed out. They will be brought in at the rate of three-a-day.
"Lt. Col. Benedict: 'It's a great plane. But our transition depends upon how soon we can get mechanics trained to keep them in flying condition.'
"As the change is being put into effect, North American Aircraft has four instructors at the base who are teaching Air Force technicians various phases of maintenance. Armament of the F-86D consists of 24 rockets in tubes under the fuselage. These are located on the underside of the aircraft in a pod. When the pilot wants to fire, the pod drops down, the rockets leave for their target, and the pod retracts again into the body. It also carries dropable wing tanks and is equipped with wing slats and brakes near the tail assembly. The Sabres will be equipped with brake chutes, a parachute which billows out behind on landing for extra safety."[7]

March: Pilots got their first taste of all-weather flying the "Dog." Six Aircraft scrambled (practice) and recovered with 200 feet and ½ mile visible. Same thing next day, only with four birds, 100 feet and ½ mile.

The primary mission of the 54th FIS with the F-86D was air defense. The squadron stood 24-hour alert as part of the 29th Air Division—24 hours on duty, then 24 hours off. If one of the ground control intercept (GCI) radar sites identified an unknown radar contact, the 54th FIS would scramble one of its alert F-86Ds to make visual contact with the unknown airborne radar contact. Most of these early interceptions were over South and North Dakota, Wyoming, and Montana. This 24-hour alert schedule was modified so alert pilots pulled either a day or night alert in 12-hour shifts, allowing for normal flight training and ground training. Even without nuclear armament on the F-86D, pilots had to show a designated pass to get on the flight line, as well as show their Air Force identification card when entering the base. Pilots could not wear their flight suits when not on the flight line. Even though the 54th FIS operated at Ellsworth AFB, their operations section was a separate facility from that of the 28th Bomb Wing.

20 March: Lt. Cook bailed out at night after fuel starvation flameout.
25 March: Maj. William H. Fairbrother relieved Col. Benedict as CO.
27 March: F-86Ds took over alert; last of the F-84s were ready to leave.
April: AIO advised the F-86D simulator will be installed in the near future.[8]

Butler Manufacturing Company architectural drawing of a four-bay aircraft alert facility designed for the United States Air Force's Air Defense Command. *Drawing from the United States Air Force Historical Research Agency at Maxwell AFB, Alabama*

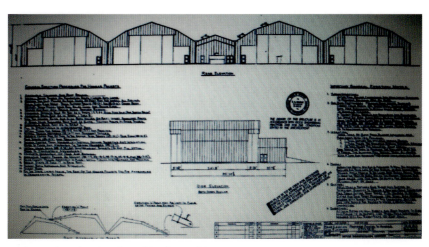

Butler engineering drawing of the front of the facility designed for the United States Air Force's Air Defense Command. *Drawing from the United States Air Force Historical Research Agency at Maxwell AFB, Alabama*

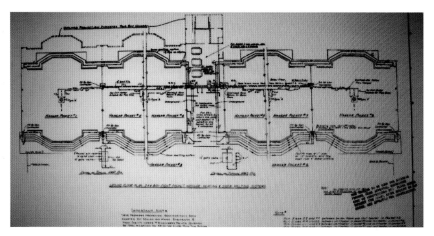

Butler engineering drawing looking down on the floor plan of the facility designed for the United States Air Force's Air Defense Command. *Drawing from the United States Air Force Historical Research Agency at Maxwell AFB, Alabama*

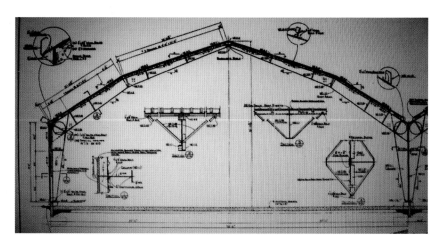

Butler engineering drawing of the front of one of the four-bays of the alert facility designed for the United States Air Force's Air Defense Command. *Drawing from the United States Air Force Historical Research Agency at Maxwell AFB, Alabama*

History of the 54th FIS

Alert bay once used by the 54th Fighter-Interceptor Squadron for its F-86Ds and F-89Js. The four hangars were moved from Ellsworth AFB for incorporation into the indoor display and office areas of the South Dakota Air and Space Museum. *Author Photo*

Inside one of the former 54th Fighter-Interceptor Squadron's aircraft alert bays. The door is covered with spray-on insulation for climate control inside the South Dakota Air and Space Museum. The missile on display is a Hound Dog air-to-ground missile carried by the Boeing B-52 Stratofortress when on alert at Ellsworth AFB. *Author Photo*

Ceiling of the alert bay showing the two tracks by which the door was raised. There were doors on either side of the hangar that allowed the aircraft to enter from one end and exit at the opposite side. *Author Photo*

The 54th Fighter-Interceptor Squadron

The *Recon Observer*, Ellsworth AFB, reported the following:

"Jet aircraft from Ellsworth AFB do not 'buzz' Rapid City at telephone level, according to Lt. H. M. West, Public Information Officer for the 54th Fighter-Interceptor Squadron. Numerous telephone calls and letters to news media and police resulted after a Sabre jet swooped over town about 8:45 p.m. last Thursday. The anonymous callers charged the plane with dangerous tactics over a thickly populated area. Lieutenant West said the only time a jet is authorized to go over the city at any time but an extremely high altitude is during an actual ADC alert, and this only happens as a last resort when normal means of communication with

F-86D inside alert hangar. Both doors are open. *South Dakota Air and Space Museum Archives*

the pilots fail. He explained a majority of the 54th pilots are on a 'back-up' basis, especially in the spring. The back-up is a standby with the pilots required to be in town, but not at the air base. Only about six pilots are at the base, the remaining are on standby."⁹

10 May: All pilots completed at least one air-to-ground rocketry mission in the F-86D for familiarization with the Pod Drop System of firing.
12 June: 2nd Lt. Arnold N. Weber bailed out from 35,000 feet after fire in an engine, no injuries.¹⁰

The *Rapid City Journal* reported the crash of an F-86D:

"An F-86D jet fighter from Ellsworth AFB, Rapid City, South Dakota, crashed and exploded in a field near Menoken [North Dakota], 10 miles east of here [Bismarck, North Dakota] shortly after noon Saturday. The pilot of the aircraft, Second Lieutenant Arnold N. Weber of El Dorado, Kansas, bailed out nearly seven miles up and parachuted to safety, coming down to earth east of Mckenzie, some ten miles away. Lieutenant Weber, who was uninjured, was assisted in his landing by a passing motorist, Joseph Swartz of Bismarck. Swartz helped Lieutenant Weber collapse his parachute and then drove him to the Bismarck airport. Meanwhile, authorities were combing the area where the plane crashed, reportedly looking for secret material or equipment supposedly to have been on the plane. A tight security guard was thrown around the crash area. Lieutenant Weber was on a routine training flight with one other jet when he heard an explosion in the rear of his plane.

"Pilot of the other Sabre was Second Lieutenant Campbell E. Prondfit, age 22, of Pikesville, Kentucky, who returned to Ellsworth AFB following the crash.

"Lieutenant Prondfit: 'I didn't know what it was. My wingman radioed from his plane. 'Son, you've got to do something. I don't know what. You'd better get out.' I tried to pull back on the throttle, but nothing happened, so I pushed the ejection button. I was catapulted into the atmosphere at 35,000 feet. I knew that if I tried to breathe I'd black out, so I held my breath as long as I could. I must have opened the chute around 15,000 feet.'

"Jack C. Pfeiffer, who farms one-half mile northwest of Menoken: 'I was dozing when the aircraft plunged into a flax field near my home. I heard the crash and then the explosion. The main body of the plane was buried in dirt and debris at the bottom of a 12-foot hole in my flax field. The wreckage was scatted over the entire field and an adjoining cornfield.'"[11]

6 July: Flying curtailed in preparation for Operation Checkpoint this month.

July: Squadron flew more than 97 sorties during Operation Checkpoint and came
    out of the exercise with two more aircraft in commission. Lt. Newell made
    a dead stick landing at Dickenson, North Dakota, after throwing several
    buckets.[12]

The *Rapid City Journal* reported on the dead stick landing by Lt. Newel:

"His officers commended Lt. William Newell in landing his powerless F-86D jet fighter at Dickinson, North Dakota, Tuesday. The fighter pilot from the 54th Fighter-Interceptor Squadron at Ellsworth AFB had engine trouble Tuesday morning while on a routine training mission over North Dakota. He was advised to land either at Dickinson or Fargo, with Lieutenant Newell deciding to land at Dickinson. Coming down to 32,000 feet, Lieutenant Newell's engine trouble increased and he cut power at about 12,000 feet. Coming in on the 1,400-foot runway, Lieutenant Newell blew both tires and was doing fine until a hay truck

Four 54th FIS F-86Ds over Mount Rushmore, South Dakota. *South Dakota Air and Space Museum Archives*

loomed in his path at the end of the strip. Lieutenant Newell veered but the plane smashed into the cab of the truck. No one was injured, but the plane and truck were damaged.

"Lieutenant Newell's superiors told him: 'His dead stick landing with a jet was a skillful feat.'"[13]

10 August: Phase II mission ran in preparation for Yuma rocketry; two T-Birds were targets.

September: Open house held for families and friends. Lt. C. E. Proudfit made a dead stick landing after turbine failure shortly after becoming airborne.

8 October: Twenty pilots and F-86Ds departed for Yuma.

5 November: Squadron returned to Ellsworth Air Force Base, 19 hits.[14]

The 54th Fighter-Interceptor Squadron

54th FIS F-89s on the parking apron. *South Dakota Air and Space Museum Archives*

History of the 54th FIS

The 54th Fighter-Interceptor Squadron

The *Rapid City Journal* reported on the 54th FIS' highly successful rocket training course:

"Home without major mishap after a concentrated 30-day course in rocket firing are members of the 54th Fighter-Interceptor Squadron under command of Major William H. Fairbrother. Leaving only a skeleton crew in the headquarters at Ellsworth Air Force Base, the 54th moved in mass in early October to Yuma, Arizona, where the Air Defense Command supervises radar-controlled interceptor training for the nation. While pilots and maintenance crews of the 54th went through the month-long training period, radar controllers on the ground are moved in and out on a two week schedule. Success of the rocket firing practice demands a radar expert on the ground relaying explicit directions to the pilot of the jet interceptor as to direction, speed, and altitude of the target. In the training at Yuma, Arizona, a SAC B-47 tows a 45-foot long target back and forth across the gunnery range. The ground controller informs the pilot as to the course of the target and directs the interceptor that way. Bringing the pilot in a flight path directly broadside of the target, which might be an enemy plane someday, is the radar controller's problem. Once the plane—whether an F-86D from the 54th or any of the American jets stationed around the nation—is headed in the right direction, the pilot used automatic gadgets built in the plane to direct his rockets for a sure hit on the target.

"Missions everyday over the Yuma Gunnery Range put every man in the interceptor squadron on his toes. Misses can be attributed to faulty radar equipment,

A T-33 on display at the South Dakota Air and Space Museum. *Author Photo*

History of the 54th FIS

Lt. Al Dalgarn, 54th FIS, in front of his F-86D on the flight line at Ellsworth AFB, 1955. *South Dakota Air and Space Museum Archives*

a plane not quite in perfect condition, misalignment of the rocket-firing equipment, or slow triggering, plus hundreds of technical faults possible in the entire set up. Hits and misses are traced to the chore assigned for every individual in the 54th and the coordination required from the radar station. Competition and practice keynote the Yuma training periods with a record number of hits per mission a constantly growing goal. Jets of the 54th returned to Rapid City, but several days will be required for return of all equipment, material, and the ground crews of the squadron."[15]

December: Squadron had two nights to work out on SAC B-47 aircraft interceptions, 112 interceptions in two nights. (The B-47s took the role of attacking Russian bombers for 54th FIS aircrews to practice interception of turbojet bombers at various altitudes, speeds, and active ECM defensive posture day, night, and in all weather.)

16 December: Four F-86Ds to Great Falls to back up the 29th Fighter Interceptor Squadron, TDY only.

1955

5 January: Six F-86Ds to Scott AFB for Operation Spotlight— night interception of B-47s.

February: About half of the squadron's F-86D-40s replaced by Operation Rollout modified F-86D-36s with drogue chutes and other improvements. All F-86D-40s to be replaced in near future.

17 February: Capt. D.C. Baker killed in a bailout attempt at low altitude after engine fire and explosion.[16]

The *Rapid City Journal* reported on the deadly crash of two F-86Ds:

"Death claimed two men from Ellsworth AFB in separate accidents on the barren prairie country 60 miles northeast of Rapid City yesterday [February 17, 1955]: Captain David E. Baker, 33, killed about 3:15 p.m., when he rode his Sabre jet too close to the ground before bailing out. The second victim was A-3C Stanislaus Countess, 17, thrown from a helicopter when it crashed at 9 p.m., en route to the scene of the jet disaster. Engine trouble was blamed for both mishaps.

"Captain Baker had radioed he was having engine trouble while on a routine mission and indicated he would try to bring the F-86D back to base. His last

Ellsworth Memorial Park, dedicated on August 20, 2000, from the Rapid City area community to those aviators who gave their lives in the performance of their duties. This marker is dedicated to Capt. David E. Baker and A-3C Stanislaus Countess who lost their lives in the service of the United States on February 17, 1955. *Author Photo*

message was that he was abandoning the plane. The ejection seat hurled him from the fighter, but apparently he had waited too long and his parachute failed to save him. Captain Baker's body was found about three miles from the wreckage of his plane. A-3C Countess was one of five men aboard the helicopter. He and others suffered minor cuts and bruises. The helicopter was being used to speed liaison between the base and the jet crash. The injured on the helicopter included Lt. Col. John Stephens, Operations Officer; Major John Malley, a B-36 aircraft commander from the 717th Bomb Squadron, 28th Bomb Wing; First Lieutenant Dean Martin, helicopter pilot; and A-1C Ernest O'Brian, 28th Air Police Squadron. Countess was assigned to the 28th Air Police Squadron. Captain Baker, a flight leader of the 54th Fighter-Interceptor Squadron at EAFB, was a Korean War veteran. He had flown 20 combat missions in Korea in F-51s. He was assigned to the 54th FIS about two years ago. A-3C Countess had been on the base only a short time.

"Blizzard weather in the open country where the planes crashed hampered recovery efforts during the night and today [February 18]. A truck and ambulance convoy started to the area during the night. The four helicopter survivors spent the night at Mud Butte and suffered no ill effects before returning home to the base, where they will get a routine medical check late this afternoon.[17]

The *Rapid City Journal* on the danger from the live rocket warheads carried by the destroyed F-86Ds:

"The two crashes were 20 miles apart. The copter hit the ground three miles east of Mud Butte, while the jet crashed two miles south of Stoneville. It was the second flight for the helicopter and apparently, the pilot had difficulty locating the jet. Before the storm moved into the area, which virtually halted all travel to the area, Major William Fairbrother, commanding officer of the 54th, had warned civilians to stay away from the scene as the jet was loaded with rockets. Gusty winds and snow moved into the area shortly before the helicopter accident."[18]

The *Rapid City Journal* on the safe return of the warheads:

"An urgent warning was issued at Ellsworth AFB today [February 23, 1955] for anyone who may have picked up rockets from the jet fighter which crashed near Stoneville last Thursday. The investigating board reported two of the rockets are missing at the scene of the crash. The rockets are equipped with a warhead designed to explode on impact. Each rocket is capable of demolishing the largest aircraft and the danger is extreme. It is possible spectators picked up the rockets as souvenirs or they may be in the field. In either case, anyone seeing the rockets should call the 54th Fighter-Interceptor Squadron at EAFB immediately."

"Residents of northeast Mead County can breathe easier now; the rocket missing from a fatal jet crash on 17 February has been discovered and detonated. All but one [initially reported as two] of the lethal rockets was recovered after the

The 54th FIS Headquarters alongside the Ellsworth AFB flight line. *South Dakota Air and Space Museum Archives*

crash. The rocket was located on the ranch of Lynn Farnham, 15 miles west of Faith. Farnham told men from the airbase and Meade County Deputy Sheriff Jim Palmer that he had picked up the rocket as a souvenir and thought it was a big shell. Farnham attempted to unscrew the bottom part of the rocket when he discovered a fuse. He had placed the rocket inside a cave about three miles from his house. Saturday, A-1C Joseph T. Munson and A-2C Max Rageth of EAFB and Sheriff Palmer went to the Farnham ranch, and he took them to the cave where the rocket was demolished. With a few taps of a hammer on the head of the rocket the story would have ended differently."[19]

The *Rapid City Journal* reported on the fourth anniversary of the 54th FIS:

"Tuesday marks the fourth anniversary of the 29th Air Division, the Air Force unit charged with defense of the five-state area, including the Dakotas, Wyoming, Nebraska, and Montana. With its nerve center at Great Falls AFB, Montana, the division controls a far-flung Ground Observer Corps network, a chain of radar stations [High Line], and all-weather jet fighter squadrons such as the 54th FIS at Rapid City. Although a part of the United States Army, units of the Antiaircraft Artillery Corps, such as the 531st Battalion at Ellsworth Air Force Base, also came under control of the 29th Air Division. The 'Ready Force' was born four years ago in the period of the Korean War when it became necessary to draw a line of defense across the northern border of the United States and along the coastline. On March 1, 1951, the 29th Air Division went into the defense business at Great Falls AFB to take care of the defenses of the five-state area.

History of the 54th FIS

Air Defense team logo at the 54th FIS headquarters. *Courtesy MSgt. Robert O'Daniel*

Members of the 54th FIS outside the headquarters building. *Courtesy Master Sgt. Robert O'Daniel*

The 54th Fighter-Interceptor Squadron

"Beginning with a handful of outdated fighters and a few radar units, it has increased its strength to include aircraft control and warning squadrons all along the High Line, all-weather jet squadrons at Rapid City and Great Falls, and Ground Observer Corps observation posts and filter centers throughout the area.

"A ground observer is a person on the ground who observes the movements of aircraft in the air. The Ground Observer Corps is a volunteer civilian organization that reports the movement of airborne aircraft to designated Air Force agencies as an aid in the detection and identification of aircraft within the air defense system. A filter center is an activity in an air defense system for receiving ground observer reports concerning flying aircraft, for evaluating, consolidating, and reconciling divergent report, and for disseminating the resulting information to an Air Defense Direction Center.

"In addition to its own capabilities, it has sister defense divisions on either side and the United States and Canada are well along the way in constructing a formidable series of radar fences stretching to the northernmost reaches of the continent.

"Brigadier General James O. Guthrie, Commanding Officer, 29th Air Division: 'It's obvious today that the shortest and most likely avenue of attack from Soviet

Members of the 1955 Ground Observer Corps during the winter near Spokane, Washington. They assisted ADC radar stations identify airborne aircraft. This was a holdover from the Ground Observers Corps of WWII along the US coastlines, especially in the Hawaiian Islands immediately after the Japanese attack on Pearl Harbor on 7 December 1944. *Courtesy Master Sgt. Robert O'Daniel*

The 54th FIS Administrative Clerk office area. *Courtesy Master Sgt. Robert O'Daniel*

Russia, should it come, would be over the polar glaciers. That puts the potential enemy just outside our backyard, and the 29th Air Division is the watchdog watching and waiting on the other side of the fence.'"[20]

March: All pilots fired air-to-ground rockets at night for familiarization.
12 April: Jo-Jo installed in neon operations building.
May: All F-86s back from Operation Pullout; improvements included new flight control system, improved radar, and a drogue chute.[21]

The *Rapid City Journal* on improvements to living conditions for the 54th FIS:

"Airmen of the 54th Fighter-Interceptor Squadron at Ellsworth AFB, who have long periods of duty on alert, are to live more comfortably. The airmen who are stationed at the squadron's alert hangar have already had their living quarters' air-conditioned, and other improvements to give them good hot meals will be made soon. Partitions have been built in their upstairs sleeping quarters to make them less barn-like and to improve heating and ventilation. The men on duty in the hangar, both pilots and ground crews, spend 24 hours at a time in the alert hangar close to their F-86D interceptors. They must be on instant readiness and have two planes in the air within five minutes of a warning to identify possible hostile aircraft. At least six pilots are on duty at all times together with crew chiefs to serve the jets, radar maintenance men, and armament men, which is a minimum of 16 men in the hangar. At present, the only facilities for eating at the hangar are a small hot plate for coffee and a refrigerator. Married men, called brown baggers, now bring their own daily lunch bags from home to last two meals. Other crewmembers have to leave the alert hangar a few at a time to obtain meals from base mess halls. Air Defense Command wants to avoid this, and at the same time make the 24-hour tour of duty as comfortable as possible. It has ordered a deep freeze which will hold pre-cooked, frozen dinners ready for the oven of a new, large electric stove. A kitchen sink, electric stove, and electronic dishwasher will be installed. Upstairs, Hollywood-type beds will replace the cots in use. Alert crews are estimated to spend 50 percent more time on duty each month under the present 24 hours on duty, 24 hours off duty schedule, than other members of the squadron. The new improvements will eventually be standard throughout the country. Men of the 54th who do alert duty welcome the changes, but laughed off the suggestion of another airman that they should get a greased fireman's pole to replace the present stairs."[22]

The current main entrance of the South Dakota Air and Space Museum. The large window above the entrance was previously the command booth that overlooked the ramp from the alert facility to the main runway. *Author Photo*

The *Rapid City Journal* on 54th FIS facility improvements:

"New improvements are now underway here on alert hangars that house the crews and Sabre jets of the 54th Fighter-Interceptor Squadron. They will enable waiting pilots and mechanics to live more comfortably during long standby periods. The 54th, a unit of the 29th Air Division (Defense), is responsible for defending the skies over the northern United States. Crews, on 24-hour duty periods, must put F-86D interceptors into the air within five minutes of a scramble bell to identify unknown airplanes. Improvements, so far, include a large air conditioner and partitions in the sleeping quarters. To be installed shortly are kitchen sinks, electric stoves, electric dishwashers, and a deep freeze to hold pre-cooked frozen dinners. Present cooking facilities include only a small hot plate and refrigerator. The new program will enable the working men to have substantial hot meals and rest without having to leave their alert buildings.

"The 54th FIS alert aircraft [four] were housed in a specially designed and constructed four-bay alert facility positioned on the southeast end of the Ellsworth AFB runway. It allowed the squadron's F-86Ds and later, F-89Js, to taxi into the alert bay through an open door in the back of the hangar. Four alert aircraft could be parked in the alert facility. A second door allowed the alert aircraft to rapidly exit, taxi to the end of the runway, and take off. In bad weather, both doors were closed to allow protection from the harsh winter temperatures and snow. Two alert bays were on either side of the center, two-story crew sleeping, ready alert crew area, and administrative/support personnel area.

"The ready alert 54th FIS aircrew, upon receiving a scramble order [Klaxon], rushed to the aircraft, climbed into the launch ready aircraft, started the engine[s], and upon receiving clearance taxied to the hold line at the end of the runway. Upon execution orders, the took off within the three-minute time launch. This was a 24-hour ready alert launch, tasked with the mission of intercepting Russian long-range bombers at high-altitude attempting to penetrate North American air space, protecting Ellsworth Air Force Base."[23]

Unlike the majority of former ADC alert facilities, the former 54th FIS four-bay facility was retained, although at a different location and operational venue. The former ADC alert facility was considered an ideal structure to house the South Dakota Air and Space Museum's growing inside displays. The Ellsworth Heritage Foundation assisted in this project, raising money and arranging for the movement of the former alert facility. In November 1988, the Foundation began discussions with the Air Force and Strategic Air Command on moving the alert bays and central connecting building from the flight to a permanent location near Ellsworth's main gate.

The $60,000 needed to move the ADC alert facility was raised through public, non-government donations. The facility was moved one bay at a

continued p 42

> time to the new location and secured to a concrete floor [foundation]. By June 1989, the museum's new facility was ready to open to the public, although not all the interior spaces had been refurbished. The former alert facility provided interior display space, gift shop, offices, and a period background for outdoor aircraft displays.

Interior of the command booth (1995) at Langley AFB. *United States Air Force Historical Research Agency*

10 June: Improvements underway on alert hangar.
24 June: Jo-Jo the lion—the 54th's mascot—was returned to Hill City Zoo.[24]

The *Rapid City Journal* on the 54th FIS' participation in the 29th Air Division's aerial rocket competition:

"Sleek, all-weather jet fighters from Ellsworth and Great Falls AFB will battle it out at 20,000 feet in early July for the right to represent the 29th Air Division in the Central Air Defense Force Rocketry eliminations in August, at Yuma, Arizona. Both fighter squadrons say they are ready and waiting for the competitive blasting that will pit planes against towed aerial targets.

F-94C Starfire on display at the National Museum of the United States Air Forces. F-94s were flown by the 29th Fighter Squadron. *Author Photo*

"Captain William J. Downey, 54th Operations Officer: 'Ellsworth fighters will begin firing July 6th and continue for three days. The top six scores registered will be sent forward and compared to those of the 29th FIS; the best team score will denote the winner.'

"Major William Fairbrother, 54th Commander: 'Of course, we'll come out on top. My men are the finest pilots in the business.'

"If the 54th team comes out with high honors, it will be ushered to Yuma, Arizona, by Captain William Norris, team leader. The 54th will begin firing at the Scenic Badlands Range, while the 29th Fighter Squadron will let loose at the Rocket Proficiency Center, Moody AFB, Georgia, beginning 11 July. The Ellsworth flyers will pilot their F-86D Sabre jets while the 29th 'Bird Men' will compete in F-94C Starfires. In the air for each squadron will be a team made up of four planes and crews plus two alternates. Forty ground personnel, including two technical representatives, will be authorized for each squadron."[25]

The 54th Fighter-Interceptor Squadron

A 54th FIS F-86D airborne from an accompanying squadron F-86D. *Courtesy Master Sgt. Robert O'Daniel*

One of the World War II two-story wood buildings used by the 54th FIS as barracks. *Courtesy Master Sgt. Robert O'Daniel*

The *Rapid City Journal* on the death of a 54th FIS pilot:

"A pilot with the 54th Fighter-Interceptor Squadron, First Lieutenant William Beasley, was killed moments after take-off from Ellsworth AFB here this morning. His Sabre jet crashed into a hilltop about a mile and a half northwest of the base, exploded, and burned a path of about 150 yards as it splattered down the far side of the grassy slope. Lieutenant Beasley was believed to be killed instantly.

"Fred Kammerer, owner of the ranch where the jet crashed: 'I heard a noise like the sound of a huge bomb exploding at 5:40 a.m. and looked out from my yard, but could see nothing. A few minutes later, the air base crash truck arrived at the scene. Wreckage of the demolished rocket-firing jet was strewn along the burned path from the top of the hill to the valley.'

"An Air Force Board of Inquiry will investigate and meanwhile, Major Walter Chance, Flying Safety officer at Ellsworth AFB: 'The crash was probably caused by mechanical failure.'

"The all-weather jet fighters stay on alert at the base around the clock and scramble to check any unidentified in the area as reported from the Filter Center and military sources. Interestingly, Lieutenant Beasley crashed near the scene of the RB-36H tragedy last August [1954] when a 26-man crew of a reconnaissance RB-36H was coming toward Ellsworth AFB for a landing. The Swallow Ranch, on which the RB-36H crashed, is south of the Kammerer Ranch."[26]

10 July: Lt. Col. Benedict left the 29th for the Air Command and Staff School.
22 July: The 29th FIS downed the 54th in rocketry competition.
27 October: 2nd Lt. McMillan landed gear up; minor aircraft damage.
16 November: Lt. Sims airlifted rare blood to ten-year-old Huron girl.[27]

The *Rapid City Journal* described the crash of an F-86D on Ellsworth's runway:

"Skidding in at 150 mph, the pilot of an F-86D Sabre jet shredded his wing tanks like coleslaw along the runway at Ellsworth AFB, but otherwise only minor damage was counted for the jet's belly landing Wednesday. Pilot Second Lieutenant Gerald P. McMillan was not injured. He had alerted the control tower that he was unable to lower the landing gear on the $460,000 aircraft and crash trucks and an ambulance were waiting at the end of his 2,500-foot skid on the north-south runway. A fire truck blew a little precautionary foam at the jet as it came to a halt."[28]

The *Rapid City Journal* reported on a 54th FIS holiday blood drive:

"Last Friday, 11 November, while many of Ellsworth and Rushmore military and civilian personnel were enjoying a holiday in observance of Veterans Day, a handful of people were busy making final arrangements for a mercy flight to Huron, South Dakota. Through the efforts of personnel from Rushmore Air Force Station (AFS), Ellsworth AFB, Ellsworth AFB Hospital, the American Red Cross,

Two F-86D tail sections on maintenance racks outside the aircraft maintenance hangar at Ellsworth AFB. *Courtesy Master Sgt. Robert O'Daniel*

The 54th FIS Operations Board—all manual updates. *Courtesy Master Sgt. Robert O'Daniel*

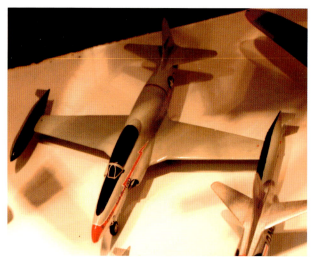

Model of a 54th FIS T-33A on display at the South Dakota Air and Space Museum. *Author Photo*

and the 54th Fighter-Interceptor Squadron, ten-year-old Dawn Dross of Hitchcock, South Dakota, a leukemia victim, has three pints of rare whole blood needed in her treatment. After the blood was taken Thursday, it was refrigerated and plans were made to fly it to Huron, South Dakota. The 54th FIS came into the picture at that point and volunteered to make the mercy flight the morning of 11 November. At 10:15 a.m., the T-33 jet trainer, with three pints of blood in the rear seat and First Lieutenant Thomas D. Sims at the controls, winged its way toward Huron and a little sick girl who will never forget the kindness of the men who gave their blood that she might have a chance for a full and healthy life."[29]

1956

5 February: The 54th returned from Yuma after thirty days of air-to-air rocketry.
15 February: Lt. Col. O. Schultz relieved Maj. Fairbrother as CO.[30]

The *Air Force Times* reported on 54th FIS rocket training via Malmstrom AFB Public Affairs:

"A news release at Malmstrom AFB, Montana states that a year of intense rocketry training is now paying dividends to the 54th Fighter-Interceptor Squadron at Rapid City, South Dakota. Twenty pilots have ganged up on aerial targets over Yuma

F-86D cocked and ready inside the alert hangar at Ellsworth AFB. *Courtesy Master Sgt. Robert O'Daniel*

AFB's Rocket Firing Range and so far have scored 91 hits. The 29th Air Division Squadron is at Yuma for its annual rocket training. So far, they have far surpassed last year's record, and when results for the final week of firing are tabulated their record is expected to soar still higher.

"Major John Clarke, Assistant Director of Plans and Requirements: 'The way we are going they should reach 150 total hits. One reason for the excellent results is the fine maintenance work. In commission rate is about 75 to 80 percent and the maintenance men are really doing a fine job. Squadron pilots highest on the scoring list: Captain William Downey (11), Captain William Norris (9), and Major William Fairbrother (7).'

"Rocket firing at Yuma simulates actual interception and destruction of enemy aircraft. When the tow target ship is in the air over the firing range, F-86D fighter-interceptors are sent aloft. The Radar Director on the ground can see on his scope both the target ship and the interceptor, and directs the fighter in much the same way he would if there were an enemy plane in the air. During intercept, team work between the pilot and Ground Director is essential. As the fighter closes in, the pilot can see the target ship on his own radar. He can also distinguish the nine by 34 foot target strung out 5,000 feet behind a SAC B-29 or B-45. Once everything is lined up, the pilot flashes in for the kill and his rockets are fired automatically."[31]

Flew in B29 to watch

The Monitor (29th Air Division [Defense]) at Malmstrom AFB reported on the 54th FIS rocket competition:

"A twinkle must have graced the eyes of four American patriots on nearby Mount Rushmore recently when a quartet of supersonic fighter pilots shot straight in the clutch to win the 29th Air Division Rocketry Championship. The 54th Fighter-Interceptor Squadron conquered the 29th FIS in a sudden death shoot-off with the 'pressure on' after the score was tied at 7,000 points at the end of the regular meet of 23 May. To determine a winner, each regular team member was allowed one final sortie over the scenic Badlands Firing Range near the Black Hills and Rapid City, South Dakota. The team with the most hits could claim the title.

"Taking first crack at the slithering six by 30 foot target sleeve behind a T-33 tow plane at 12,000 feet was the 29th FIS. The pilot [Captain Jack Butterfield] and radar-observer [Lieutenant John La Marr] ripped a hole in it, but the rest of the team retired without scoring, leaving the 54th behind with a one hit deficit. First pilot up for the 54th was Lieutenant Geme Levy, who had already scored three hits in the regular meet. On his first pass 24 rockets shot toward the target, but all missed. Major Robert Highsmith, the second man with a chance to tie the score, shot a hole right through the center of the banner, leaving two 54th FIS pilots the chance to win the meet. Captain William Norris, with four hits already under his belt, clinched the title for his team with another perfectly placed rocket. Lest there be a doubt, Lieutenant Dennis Winkels, in his final turn, neatly shot off the target.

"The final victory was but one of a series of climaxes in an aerial battle as close, hard-fought, and tense as a match between Joe Lewis and Jack Dempsey

Four 54th FIS F-86Ds airborne in line formation.
Courtesy Master Sgt. Robert O'Daniel

The 54th FIS mobile control tower. *Courtesy Master Sgt. Robert O'Daniel*

night have been. Twice before the regular meet was over the score was tied, and no more than two hits ever separated the two teams. One of the most dramatic moments in the meet came when a pair of 29th FIS sharpshooters, Lieutenants Danny Parris and Daniel Kinsella, splattered the target in a last ditch effort to tie the 54th on the final day of regular shooting. The 54th led 7,800 to 6,800 and had two make-up sorties to go. The 29th, trailing by one hit, had but one attempt left. Parris and Kinsella fired first. Their goal was to score a hit on the first pass or the meet was lost. They lined up their F-94C Starfire dead on the 90-degree beam attack, and from the '20 seconds to go' signal, not a single correction was necessary. Careful investigation of the target by the airborne judge and aerial photographer revealed one rocket had neatly pierced the target's center. With the score tied at 7,800 apiece, the pressure was on. For the two FIS pilots, a hit by either would pull the meet out of a tie.

"However, the win by the 54th entitles them to represent the 29th Air Division at the Central Air Defense shoot-off in Yuma, Arizona, in mid-July. Major William Lewis, Division Fighter Officer: 'Their planes are in excellent shape and their pilots are well trained and highly qualified. We know there are other good teams in CADF, but we feel sure the 54th will win. The way they came through at the end, with three hits in four tries, when the pressure was really on, gives us a good idea what they can do.'"[32]

6 May: Maj. Fairbrother left for England.
21 May: The 54th will carry 29th Air Division colors to the CADF shoot off at Yuma.
July: Computer fuses plagued the 54th, finish CADF meet in sixth slot.
August: Col. Marshall's CADF tactical evaluation team complimented the 54th.
    Maj. Lane flew cobra serum to cobra bite victim New Orleans youth.
4 October: Lt. Kowal made a successful low-level ejection after compressor failure.[33]

"Fighter pilot bails to safety, jet sets fire in Rapid Valley," *Rapid City Daily Journal*, Rapid City, South Dakota, October 4, 1956:

What started as a routine mission for a jet fighter pilot at Ellsworth Air Force Base this morning (October 4, 1956) wound up in near disaster. Slightly injured after "hitting the silk" when he felt the tail of his F-86D fighter-interceptor explode was Second Lieutenant Glenn Kowal. He was flying at about 7,000 feet at the time of the mishap [9:45 a.m.]. Lieutenant Kowal landed about one mile and a half from the crash scene and was picked up by three neighborhood youths who were attracted by the smoke. They were met by a base fire truck, which took Lieutenant Lowal to the hospital for a medical check. The grass fire which started when the jet plane hit the ground six miles southeast of Rapid City was controlled after a resident called the air base and the local fire department.

History of the 54th FIS

Buick outside the 54th FIS alert hangar (back side) after a light snowfall. *Courtesy Master Sgt. Robert O'Daniel*

Base firemen arrived at the scene in short order and with Rapid City firemen and rancher volunteers had the grass fire surrounded.

Another problem was to hold sightseers away from the plane, which carries 16 loaded rockets. They are electrically detonated from the plane, but the warheads are constructed to explode on contact. Souvenir hunters were warned not to touch any of the lethal weapons, which were strewn around the field.

The plane, at 9:50 a.m., three miles west of the Rapid City Municipal Airport, plummeted into the ground on the Charles Bradsky ranch in Rapid Valley. The location is approximately four miles south of the beef dump station on Highway 40, east of Rapid City. There were no buildings within a mile of the spot where the plane smashed. Officers of the 54th under command of Colonel Herbert O. Schulze started an investigation of the incident immediately. However, no details were available. Pilots in the F-86Ds wear a parachute pack and are sitting on an ejection seat. Pushing the "panic button" throws the plastic canopy off the jet and the pilot is then hurled up and away from his abandoned plane. The parachute is released manually by the pilot after he is clear of the aircraft.[34]

The 54th Fighter-Interceptor Squadron

1957

1957–1960, the squadron flew the Northrop F-89J Scorpion.

January: Maj. Alma R. Flake relieved Lt. Col. Schulze as CO.
1 March: Maj. Flake led a 12-ship deployment to Great Falls, Casper, Sioux City, Lincoln, and returned; no aborts.
April: Eighteen pilots qualified as the 54th fired air-to-air missiles on the Badlands Range.
5 May: The 54th ended a 39-day alert at Malmstrom as the 29th FIS transitioned to the F-89H.
12 June: Inclement weather forced the postponement of CADF tactical evaluation.
22 June: The 54th scored 109 hits in two weeks of rocketry at Wendover AFB, Utah.
10 July: Five F-86Ds sent to Iran as the first step in F-86D phase out.[35]

The 54th FIS commander Lt. Col. Alma R. Flake (far left) re-enlisting three members of the squadron in his office. At far right is Sgt. Robert O'Daniel. *Courtesy Master Sgt. Robert O'Daniel*

The *Rapid City Journal* on the top secret involvement of two 54th FIS pilots during US atomic bomb tests:

"Two pilots from the 54th Fighter-Interceptor Squadron at Ellsworth AFB participated in the recent series of A-bomb tests in Las Vegas, New Mexico, by flying through atomic radiation areas for 30 minutes. The two, Lieutenant Billy B. Coggin and Second Lieutenant Robert F. Waggoner, participated in the exercise to demonstrate safety measures taken to safeguard humans during the atomic blasts. Coggin and Waggoner ferried a T-33 from EAFB to Nellis AFB and later to Yucca Flats, testing site for 'Operation PLUMBBOB.' On 24 July, they took-off at 4:50 a.m. and planned the flight so they would be in a designated position five minutes before the atomic device to be detonated in a T-33.

"At 'zero hour' when the blast occurred, they were leading a flight of six planes about 60 minutes from the explosion. Two seconds before the blast, they lowered their heads into the cockpit and kept them there for six seconds. Looking up four seconds after the detonation, they were able to see the huge atomic fireball rising into the sky. For 30 minutes after the blast they flew a holding pattern in the area. After the half hour was up, the flight flew through the cloud in trail formation, wearing only standard flight gear. Lieutenants Coggin and Waggoner said their first view after the detonation showed a dark, reddish-brown cloud rising 20,000 feet above the desert. After flying through the cloud, the two lieutenants returned to Nellis AFB and underwent tests for radioactivity. The A-bomb was classified as a 'medium yield' weapon.

"The two lieutenants after their test flight indicated they received an insignificant radioactive dose. According to plan, the T-33 was held until the next morning before it was permitted to return to Ellsworth AFB. The lieutenants expressed complete confidence in their capability to operate a similar weapon if the need becomes necessary."[36]

For Operation PLUMBBOB, with the establishment of the 4950th Test Group (nuclear) at the Air Force Special Weapons Center on September 1, 1956, the 4926th Test Squadron (sampling) became part of that group. The primary mission of the 4950th Test Group during Operation PLUMBBOB was to provide limited support and control the aircraft necessary to collect and record data by the participating services, command, and the Atomic Energy Commission.

Planning Directive 3-56 gave the Test Aircraft Unit responsibility for test operational flying activities, particularly: (1) test area briefing, (2) control of sampler and cloud aircraft, (3) radiological and weather reconnaissance flights, (4) providing some maintenance facilities at Indian Springs, and (5) coordinating take-off and landing schedules. Four T-33 aircraft were assigned to sampling missions. The T-33s staged from Nellis AFB. The atomic detonations for assigned EAFB T-33 involvement was on July 24, 1957, during "Shot Kepler," an atomic device mounted and detonated on top of a 500-foot tall steel tower.[37]

Northrop F-89J Scorpions assigned to the 54th Fighter-Interceptor Squadron on the flight line at Ellsworth AFB. *Courtesy Master Sgt. Robert O'Daniel*

The *Black Hills Bomber* (Ellsworth AFB) on the inspection of the 54th FIS:

"Next week, a unique inspection will take place at the 54th Fighter-Interceptor Squadron. A special inspection team led by Col. Winton Marshall will arrive here Monday for a week long check. The inspection by the Central Air Defense Forces' Tactical Evaluation Team regularly checks fighter interceptor and aircraft control and warning squadrons through the 19-state area for combat efficiency. Col. Marshall: 'They fly in all types of weather and under various simulated combat conditions to check the combat flying crews of the Force.'

"Special equipment is used to evaluate the techniques and proficiency of the crews being tested, including radarscope recorders and midget tape recorders. Tape readers used for this type mission are small enough to be carried in the flying suit of the pilot. Comments of the evaluator and moving pictures of the mission are used to explain in detail the errors of personnel taking the test.

"Expert controllers of the Tactical Team evaluate the work of squadron personnel during a simulated combat mission and read the radarscope with the man under examination. Written tests are given to all members of the aircrews and controllers. Moving pictures of the flight are also studied and techniques evaluated. Flying on the wingtip of the interceptor being tested, the team member in an F-86D aircraft completes the whole mission. Frequently, there are 12 to 15 planes participating in the exercises.

"Col. Marshall: 'We encounter real competition from the boys of the fighter-interceptor squadrons. And, we also learn a lot from the exercises. Ideas and suggestions of real value frequently come from the GCI operations, the all-important men who set up the aircrews for the attack on the target.'

"Standardization of individual interceptor squadrons with the ADC is required to insure the complete mobility of flying units. Each squadron is checked to insure standard procedures, but in CADF the Marshall team goes further by checking on intercept techniques, time taken to refuel after a mission, knowledge by each man of his specific task, and the way he performs under simulated combat conditions. During the test, interceptor aircraft travel at rates as high as 800 mph with the pilot, at all times, under simulated instrument conditions. Colonel Marshall and his men do not 'follow the weather.' They are often caught in desert heat in July or northern blasts in December."[38]

16 August: Tactical evaluation proveed the 54th to be one of CADF's top units, primarily as a result of outstanding rocketry and subsequent evaluations.
August: Col. Marshall submited Capt. Norris and Capt. Levy for "expert" rating.
September: The 54th to Great Falls to pull alert for the 29th.
October: The 54th missed first place in CADF rocket meet due to bad wing film. Capt. Norris took individual honors in the CADF rocket meet.
28 October: First day of F-89J MTD for 54th pilots.
10 November: First F-89J arrived to replace the F-86D.

Four-bay Air Defense Command aircraft alert hangars at the end of the runway at Ellsworth AFB. Note the original color compared to the painted color on the hangars after they moved to the South Dakota Air and Space Museum. *South Dakota Air and Space Museum*

December: Squadron transitioned from the F-86D to the F-89J.
19 December: Newly assigned air policemen arrived to take charge of guarding Special Weapons Section.[39]

In a letter from Headquarters ADC to Commander 54th Fighter-Interceptor Squadron, Ellsworth AFB, South Dakota, dated November 1, 1957.

1. On October 27, 1957, the 54th Fighter-Interceptor Squadron completed a one-year accident free period. It is noted that you were in command of this organization from February 1, 1957, to October 27, 1957.
2. By designing safety of operation into your operation, you have maintained an excellent period in your unit and have increased the effectiveness of the Air Defense Command. Your achievement is symbolic of more than just a safety record. Through your leadership, you developed the necessary teamwork to assure maximum operational capability.
3. In view of this, it gives me a great deal of pride and pleasure to commend you for a mission carried in the finest Air Force tradition. It not only reflects much credit upon yourself and your organization, but upon the United States Air Force as a whole.[40]

F-89J of the 54th FIS in front of a maintenance hangar at Ellsworth AFB. *South Dakota Air and Space Museum Archives*

The 54th Fighter-Interceptor Squadron

1958

In early May 1958, with the conversion to the F-89J completed and the squadron fully alert and combat ready, the 54th FIS settled down to undertake its full training schedule. The squadron's flying time had averaged well over 600 hours per month since April (April 608 hours, May 666 hours, and June 715 hours). Flight time was hampered by the aircraft's air compressors, which required maintenance to maintain flight training schedules. The conversion from F-86Ds to F-89Js required thirteen weeks of training command school on power ground equipment scheduled to begin on July 23.

Maintenance was a continuing transition from the F-86D to the F-89J. The squadron's Airframe Shop operated with six personnel who had completed the required on-the-job training on the F-89J, but three of these personnel were scheduled to be transferred to another unit or discharged from active duty, thereby placing the maintenance activities of the Airframe Shop at an operational level that would impact F-89J operations. This shop had accomplished approximately 475 work orders during June with one T-33 under repair, damaged by a plenum explosion.

The squadron's engine shop was heavily tasked to maintain the new aircraft. The shop had an in-house strength of twenty-eight men at various training levels. The engine shop completed seventeen periodic inspections on F-89J aircraft engines and three periodic inspections on T-33A aircraft engines. At this time the squadron had reached full strength with 28 F-89Js, 3 T-33As, 84 officers, and 473 airmen. Even with new training and loss of personnel, the squadron maintained a six-day working time on aircraft maintenance inspections. Aircraft out of commission for parts (AOCF) had reached a maximum of 33 days, with one F-89J grounded for eighteen days pending the delivery of a fuel pump.

The transition from F-86Ds to F-89Js progressed fairly well in spite of supply shortages and continued spotty supply action, particularly with respect to the base unit. Bench stocks and pre-issued levels were rapidly attaining authorized levels—not unusual with new Air Force weapons systems, as production of new aircraft proceeded spare parts production and entrance into the maintenance supply chain. Some areas in the squadron were over-manned with the transition from the F-86D to the F-89J. It took time for the necessary skill levels of squadron personnel to reach desired levels to maintain F-89Js in the squadron.

On April 1, 1958, Squadron Operations had reached a strength of 36 pilots and 30 radar observers, all ADC alert certified. During June, the squadron lost three pilots and gained eight, lost eight radar observers, and gained six for a month end total of 34 pilots and 31 radar observers. Maintaining qualified radar observers in ADC squadrons was a continuous problem.

With the conversion to F-89Js, the squadron operated its own Air Police Section to guard special weapons (Genie air-to-air missiles armed with a 1.5 kiloton nuclear fission warhead). As of June, the squadron had nine Genie AAMS, although it was authorized thirteen. (It can be assumed the squadron would have one nuclear fission warhead for each missile to meet ADC alert standards.) Starting in July 1958, the squadron's air police (36 assigned) assumed primary security duties for guarding Genie AAMs and their nuclear fission warheads.

The air police attached to the squadron in 1958 was the first unit in ADC to be equipped and use walkie-talkies in its security operations, an improved version of Motorola electronics communications equipment.

The squadron's Special Weapons Section (those who handled Genie missiles and particularly the fission nuclear warheads) had a strength of six personnel trained in these weapon systems and support by base fire department personnel to deal with such munition crash hazards associated with these nuclear warheads if mated to an aircraft.

The Ellsworth AFB ADC Special Weapons Storage area was completed in early June, inspected, and turned over to the squadron on June 24. Nuclear weapons required extensive intrusion alarm protection, and all personnel learned the alarm's capabilities and operation. All buildings in the secure area were controlled by air police and numbered for rapid response if and when an alarm was triggered. The security for nuclear weapons was absolute, given the wide deployment of such weapons on Air Force bases in the United States.[41]

26–29 May: Inspector General of Central Air Defense Force conducted inspection of squadron, rated excellent.[42]

"The role played by the ADC, of which the 54th Fighter-Interceptor Squadron at Ellsworth AFB is a component, was particularly explained for the Kiwanis Club of Rapid City by Lt. Col. A. R. Flake, commanding officer of the jet outfit. Lt. Col. Flake traced, briefly, the way most nations have rejected advanced military ideas, and suffer subsequently, before expanding on present and potential weapons for the United States. Timed with celebration of Armed Forces Day in Rapid City, the colonel's explanation touched on radar warning systems this nation has developed to alert both the defense weapons and the retaliatory weapons as embodied by SAC's new bombers. The entire program is geared to the theme that our retaliatory strength could not be completely destroyed and the enemy is going to suffer in his homeland. The fighter-interceptor aircraft now in use can meet the enemy far away from vital bomber bases such as Ellsworth. Guided missiles are being developed that are more effective than the Nikes for Ellsworth AFB and somewhere in the globe there are bombers that can make a destructive strike on the nation that attacks us. Lt. Col. Flake: 'They can't destroy everything if we continue to develop our program.'"[43] (*Rapid City Journal*)

The *Rapid City Journal* on the 54th FIS picnic at Canyon Lake Park in Rapid City:

"Weather or not, rain or shine, the 54th Fighter-Interceptor Squadron will hold its annual picnic this year in Rapid City's Canyon Lake Park. What is expected to be the biggest and best of the 54th annual picnics is set for Saturday from 11

Russian Air Force Long-Range Aviation Tupolev Tu-95 Bear heavy, strategic (conventional and nuclear bomber). This was the Russian bomber Air Defense Command would try to intercept after launch from Soviet Northern Arctic staging bases, flying over the North Polar region, across Canada, and into the United States. The bomber remains on active duty, as does Air Combat Command's Boeing B-52H Stratofortress. *United States Air Force*

a.m. to 4 p.m., and according to Park Superintendent Merle Gunderson, the park will be closed to the public from 8 a.m. to 8 p.m.

"Lt. Col. A.R. Flake, commanding officer of the 54th: 'The annual gathering of men and families of the squadron had grown to where we expect between 1,200 to 1,500 picnickers and we're going all out on this one. I hope this year that the squadron picnic will surpass anything of previous years.' Gunderson explained that as an experiment the park and all facilities would be closed for the exclusive use of the 54th. As far as he knows, it is the first time the entire park has been taken over by a group. At the request of Lt. Col. Flake, and with the consent of the Rapid City Mayor and City Council, the closing of the park to the public is an experiment. Gunderson pointed out there are other parks in the city with similar facilities including rest rooms, picnic stoves, and garbage areas. He recommended local citizens make use of Roosevelt or one of the other parks on Saturday.

"Entertainment will include music by the Ranch Hands, an air base western combo; a softball game between the officers and enlisted men at 1 p.m.; and a horseshoe tournament and other adult games thought up on the spur of the moment. The 54th Wives Club is in charge of games for the children. Refreshments, already purchased and stockpiled, will be provided by the squadron and the Wives Club. Air police will assist in directing traffic and parking vehicles."[44]

24 June: CWO Hudson took over new completed ADC Special WSA. (This was an unusual, unclassified, open source reference validating that nuclear weapons were being stored at Ellsworth AFB.)
26 June: First "Dining-In" held. Guest speaker was Maj. Gen. Alfred E. Kolberer.
11 July: Deployed to Vincent AFB, Arizona, for weapons training.

16 July: Returned to Ellsworth without completing training due to international situation and increased alert commitment.[45]

Letter of commendation from Headquarters Central ADC to Commander, 54th Fighter-Interceptor Squadron.

1. It is a real pleasure to forward General Bowman's commendation to you.
2. Mobility and flexibility have been inherent characteristics of the Air Force since its inception. However, progressive developments in aircraft and supporting equipment during the last decade have created implications requiring expert planning, sound judgment, and skilled personnel in order to retain these elements essential to the tactical application of air power.
3. Notwithstanding the fact that twelve of your twenty-two aircraft were airborne on the gunnery range at the time you received word to execute an unscheduled redeployment, all aircraft were airborne in less than three and one-half hours and twenty-one aircraft completed the redeployment, without incident, in less than six hours. The one remaining aircraft met the redeployment take-off as scheduled but was required to return to Vincent AFB, where an engine change was expeditiously accomplished. This aircraft arrived at Ellsworth AFB in less than nine hours after the return of the main body of your squadron.
4. This outstanding accomplishment reflects a high degree of skill and esprit de corps. It would not have been possible without the fullest cooperation among all participating personnel. Please express my personal congratulation and sincere appreciation to all members of your squadron for a job well done.[46]

21 August: The squadron participated in an exercise against the 28th Bombardment Wing's B-52s. (The squadron's F-89Js simulated attacks against large turbojet bombers as they would be tasked to intercept and shoot down Russian Air Force bombers. The SAC aircrews used their ECM to counter and confuse the approaching 54th FIS fighters.)

11 September: Participated in an exercise against the 28th Bombardment Wing's B-52s, which were using extensive ECM. (It was expected penetrating Russian Air Force bombers would use some form of ECM to conceal their location and confuse interception by ADC fighters. SAC's ECM capabilities were probably somewhat higher than those of the Russian Air Force and provided the 54th FIS pilots as close to a possible real war scenario of airborne interception of turbojet bombers at high altitude and high speed.)

16 September: Visit to the squadron by Maj. Gen. Stevenson, commander of the 29th Air Division, and Brig. Gen. Neely, commander of the 29th Air Division.

19–20 September: Exercise Top Hand.

25 September: Central Air Defense Force tactical evaluation.

22 October–13 November: The squadron participated in six training exercises in preparation for ADC Operational Readiness Inspection.

F-89Js of the 54th FIS airborne in formation. *South Dakota Air and Space Museum Archives*

3-7 November: ADC Inspector General conducted weapons inspection.
6-7 November: CDAF tactical evaluation of the squadron.[47]

In September 1958, the squadron's monthly report stated that prior to July 1958, it had made extensive plans and carried on a special flying program in preparation for the tactics that the squadron was expected to use when deployed to Vincent AFB, Arizona, on July 11, 1958, for weapons training. (It took time to write the report from such an exercise, usually a thirty-day reporting requirement to higher headquarters, 29th Air Division. The report provides a look at the training required by an ADC F-89J unit for conventional warhead armed air-to-air missiles when on standard ADC alert.) The squadron arrived as scheduled in Arizona and flew 24 sorties on July 15 on the weapons firing range. Twelve sorties were flown the next day. The remaining 12 sorties were cancelled when the squadron was ordered to return to Ellsworth AFB as soon as possible to assume an increased alert commitment.

The squadron received a letter of appreciation and commendation from Headquarters Central Air Defense Force for the expeditious and professional manner in which the deployment was accomplished. It was assumed the squadron would return to Vincent AFB in November 1958 to resume its weapons training.

The squadron coordinated two exercises with the 28th BW at Ellsworth AFB (SAC). On August 21, eleven profile missions were flown against a 28th BW B-52. The B-52 was flying a simulated Russian Air Force bomber penetration flight into the northern United States, providing high-altitude, high-subsonic speed interception of a modern turbojet bomber. Nine of these intercept missions were classified as successful (82%). The two unsuccessful profiles were due to the effectiveness of the electronic countermeasures (ECM) employed by the B-52's electronic officer. On September 11, fourteen profile missions were flown against a second 28th BW B-52. Nine of these missions (64%) were successful. The unsuccessful profiles were due to errors on the part of aircrews and ground control intercept (GCI) directors. Electronic countermeasures were ineffective during this exercise. All of these profiles were single firing passes conducted in strict accordance with established ADC procedures and regulations. These exercises proved to be of great benefit to the squadron's aircrews, as they were able to fly against aircraft employing ECM. Additionally, the bomber crews had the opportunity to test their ECM capability against attacking fighters.

During September, the Northern Air Defense Exercise Top Hand was conducted September 19–20. A Central Air Defense Force exercise was conducted on September 25 and 21 sorties were flown. The evaluation of the squadron's performance in this exercise had not been received by the squadron as of September.[81]

On September 12, 1958, an F-89J piloted by 1st Lt. Richard E. Smith, 54th FIS, Ellsworth AFB, sloshed and skidded down the foam-covered runway of Malmstrom AFB in a remarkable display of cool thinking and precision flying. With his scissors joint sheared and the right landing gear cocked at a 60 degree angle, Lt. Smith, 26, of Albuquerque, New Mexico, and his radar observer, 1st Lt. Richard P. Ryan, 24, of St. Louis, Missouri, brought the twenty-two ton fighter home undamaged. So smooth was their landing they neither blew the right tire nor inflicted any further damage to the wheel or gear assembly. One hour and fifty minutes earlier, on take-off roll, Lt. Smith noticed a constant buffeting prior to his wheels leaving the ground. Insufficient runway necessitated the take-off be completed. The buffeting ceased when airborne, but when the gear was raised an unsafe warning light flashed red on the instrument panel. Lt. Smith leaned forward to check the gear visually but could not see anything of immediate concern, since his field of vision was limited by the design of the aircraft. After trying again unsuccessfully to recycle the landing gear, Lt. Smith requested the tower to contact Col. Nolkamper, director of Operations and Training at 29th Air Division Headquarters; John Cianfringe, technical representative for North American Aviation, designated to the F-89J; and 1st Lt. Donald L. Rouze, a fellow pilot, for a visual check.

After four flybys the cocked condition of the landing gear was noted. By leaning as far forward as possible, Lt. Smith also spotted the break in the scissors (a set of torque arms—two pieces of metal or other material—hinged together to form an elbow serving to allow the parts to telescope but preventing them from turning around). It was decided by the tower and Lt. Smith to attempt a "bump and go" touchdown at 140 knots—20 knots over landing speed—to try and straighten the cocked landing gear. This proved unsuccessful. Lt. Smith then dumped his tip tank fuel and circled the field for an hour and forty minutes with his speed brakes open and his engine at 100 percent RPM to burn maximum fuel. During this time Lt. Ryan was coaching Lt. Smith on ideal landing speeds and emergency procedures.

When the fuel load had decreased to 2,500 pounds and the fire department had laid a blanket of foam 5,000 feet long and 24 feet wide on the right side of the runway, Lt. Smith began his descent and touchdown. Skillfully, despite a hydraulic leak that made operation of flaps and speed brakes painfully slow, the pilot maintained the right main gear on the foam while the left main gear on the nose wheel stayed on the dry surface. Steering was accomplished by the nose wheel and left brake. The aircraft traveled 7,400 feet before coming to a halt and out jumped two of the happiest guys in the world.

Lts. Smith and Ryan were recommended by Lt. Col. Alma R. Flake, commander, 54th FIS, for the US Air Force's "Well Done Award" and the ADC's "We Point with Pride Award." Their achievement was all the more remarkable considering Lt. Smith only had 53 flying hours in the F-89J at the time.[48]

17–21 November: ADC Operational Readiness Inspection and tactical evaluation.
28 November–19 December: Squadron deployed to Vincent AFB, Arizona, for weapons training. The squadron broke thirty-one world records during this period.

54th Fighter-Interceptor Squadron Awards and Records Since 1953

Date	Award
3 September 1953–3 March 1954	ADC six month Flying Safety
14 July 1954–14 January 1955	ADC six month Flying Safety
7 July–7 January 1956	ADC six month Flying Safety
27 October 1956–27 April 1957	ADC six month Flying Safety
27 October 1956– 27 October 1957	ADC twelve month Flying Safety
1 July 1958– 30 June 1959	USAF Flying Safety
1 July 1958–30 June 1959	Hughes Achievement Award
1 October 1958–October 1959	ADC twelve month Flying Safety
August 1959	Aircraft Gas Turbine Engine Maintenance Certificate of Recognition
1 November 1958– 31 December 1958	CADF "A" Award for Outstanding Performance during a Tactical Evaluation by the Defense Force Tactical Evaluation Team[49]

In early October 1958, the squadron began an intensive program of crew training—via actual flying and ground training conducted by the squadron radar observer—to increase the effectiveness of the F-89J against targets flying below an absolute altitude of 5,000 feet. (It was assumed Russian Air Force bombers would follow SAC bomber crews' low-level penetration tactics to fly low, below current Russian radar minimum altitude tracking, using terrain masking to penetrate into heavily defended targets.) For most of the radar observers, this was their first exposure to the difficulties encountered in low-altitude interceptions; a change from their standard high-altitude attack profiles. The MG 12 Fire Control System was not designed to operate at such altitudes, but with increased training the proficiency of the aircrews increased. This low altitude training was a significant factor toward the squadron's high success rate during the ASC Operational Readiness Inspection (ORI) in November. This is a good example of the degree to which an ADC fighter-interceptor squadron had to meet high operational standards to qualify to perform interception of hostile/unidentified targets over the United States.[50]

The 54th FIS also participated in several 29th AD training exercises in October and November 1958 used to demonstrate the squadron's ability to intercept airborne hostile threats.

Date of exercise	Interception Success Rate
22 October	77%
27 October	70%
30 October	69%
6 November	72%
7 November	66%
13 November	76%

This indicated that against a perceived enemy threat, approximately 30% of an attacking bomber force would break through a conventionally armed air-to-air missile attack.

An ADC weapons inspection of the 54th FIS was conducted on November 3–7, 1958. The Central Air Defense Force (CADF) inspection team conducted a thorough Tactical Evaluation of the squadron. During this evaluation, 48 profile missions were attempted and 40 were successful (83%). Of the 71 intercepts attempted 50 were successful (70%):[51]

> During November 17–21, a Tactical Evaluation/Operational Readiness Inspection of the 54th FIS was conducted by representatives of headquarters, ADC. The evaluators stated that the 84% success rate established by the squadron during this ORI against targets of varying speeds and altitudes, including very low altitudes, was well above the average ADC fighter squadron. This intensive aircrew training against low altitude targets increased the effectiveness of the squadron to intercept hostile targets attempting to slide under radar sites to penetrate North American airspace.

54th FIS aircrews were found to be aggressive and well qualified in air defense tactics. Except for some modified spacing between flights, ADC profiles were strictly adhered to. It was noted that in some cases the F-89J pilots became overly aggressive and regulated airspeed or altitude changes before required to do so by the weapons director. Air discipline was excellent and pilot steering was termed "the best yet observed by the evaluation team."

An area of great weakness—previously known to the squadron and throughout the division—stressed by the evaluation team is ineffective means of ground communication between the 54th FIS and its associated AC&W [Aircraft Control and Warning] squadrons. A more effective means of communication is necessary for critiquing northern sites after missions. Inspectors realize that a good communication is necessary for developing a closer relationship between AC&W squadrons and ADC. The unsatisfactory communication system is due to the limited number of telephone circuits and the excessive voice attenuation on the available circuits. This is a problem throughout the divisions. A program to improve this situation is in progress.

The evaluation team also encourages, as soon as possible, the resumption of cross training with the 740th AC&W Squadron, also situated at Ellsworth AFB. This has been impossible during this reporting period as the 740th AC&W Squadron was undergoing major equipment changes. ADC plans to resume cross training immediately. In addition, the squadron is planning to have aircrews visit the remote northern sites in the 29th AD. In this way aircrews will become more familiar with the operations of these sites and the ground controllers, many of whom are not aircrew members, will be briefed on the problems encountered in this "flying game."

The evaluators were impressed with the effective coordination between the 54th FIS, Ellsworth AFB, and Civil Aeronautics Administration agencies. The evaluator felt the expeditious clearing of aircraft for instrument departures and arrivals contributed greatly to the success of the exercise. [This was a practice to demonstrate regardless of weather conditions, the squadron's F-89Js could take off, intercept hostile airborne targets, land back at Ellsworth, and be turned around for another sortie if required.] During the inspection, squadron flying safety was found to be excellent. But it was pointed out that ground operation on the Ellsworth aircraft ramp would be improved if wing walkers were assigned to aircraft taxiing through congested ramp areas. [Interestingly, this is what ground personnel did at fighter fields in England during WWII when aircraft were parked everywhere and congestion was a problem.]

Maintenance on squadron aircraft during this time period was found to be quite satisfactory. During the exercise, the average operational ready rate was 82% with the squadron's 28 F-89Js. The average in-commission rate for the F-89Js' fire control system was 95% for both days of the exercise. Average radar observer identification of an airborne target was 25.1 nautical miles and the average lock on was 14.5 nautical miles. The evaluation team said this was well above average for this type of equipment. As a result of the inspection, the 54th FIS was declared capable of performing its mission:

> The primary mission of the 54th Fighter Interceptor Squadron is to achieve and maintain a level of operation effectiveness which will enable it to intercept and destroy enemy aircraft and/or airborne weapons. The 54th Fighter Interceptor Squadron will keep prepared to participate in the collateral mission and in support of other US and allied command as directed or appropriate.[52]

In a letter from Headquarters 29th Air Division (Defense, ADC), United States Air Force, Malmstrom AFB, Montana, "Commendation," to Commander, 54th Fighter-Interceptor Squadron, Ellsworth AFB, South Dakota, December 15, 1958.

1. During the recent ORI [November 17–21, 1958], you and your organization were recognized by the ORI team, myself, and staff for accomplishing the mission in an outstanding manner.
2. I wish to commend you and your personnel for a job well done and the superior leadership by you, your officers, NCOs, and airmen.
3. The excellent results obtained by your organization reflect the continuous effort and hard work you and your personnel put forth. I am certain this could not have been accomplished without the esprit de corps your organization had always displayed under your leadership.
4. I am confident the 54th can accomplish its ADC mission and it will continue in effectiveness under the leadership of you and your personnel.
5. Please express my appreciation to your personnel of a job well done.[53]

The Ellsworth AFB newspaper reported the following:

Around Rapid City, Deadwood, and points northwest, there's just one way to deal with killers and spoilers of peace: that's with the 54th Fighter-Interceptor Squadron and the smell of jet smoke. Proficiency is their watchword. No less than peak performance is tolerated, whether among or with maintenance personnel. Outsiders who stop to watch are immediately impressed with the cool, calculated efficiency of the ground crews in a weapons loading exercise or the poised, confident, business-like manner of the pilots and their radar observers as they run up their 22-ton fighters and head them down the runway toward unknown targets.

Model of a Northrop F-89J on display at the South Dakota Air and Space Museum with 54th FIS markings. *Author Photo*

The men, guided by their commander, Lt. Col. Alma R. Flake, proved their worth and dependability late last month when they streaked across the Arizona skies to shatter 28 global records of the Air Defense Command. After completing the 21-day missile meet at Vincent AFB, Arizona, the squadron returned to Ellsworth with first place honors for the command, defeating the 47 other bases represented. A few of the evaluations included: assembly and loading of weapons, scramble procedures, firing accuracy, maintenance, and launching of weapons. In each of these and 22 other ratings, the 54th settled for no less than the best record. Through the desert skies the Ellsworth jets streaked with precision operation, showing the nation they were capable of their positions: ready to deliver their scientific and deadly serious type of warfare.

These pilots need not see their targets; modern equipment sees it for them. Once alerted, the pilot takes to the air and is vectored by ground radar to a target rendezvous. Direction, altitudes, and speed of the attacking aircraft are reduced to known components before the actual firing run even begins. Once the target is electronically sighted, digital computers grind out attack information, display it to the aircrews, and within seconds the approaching enemy aircraft is reduced to ashes and cosmic dust.

Unlike other branches of the US armed forces who "move on their stomach," the fighter outfit moves on its maintenance. Maintenance becomes the nucleus around which the success of the squadron must rotate. Hundreds of details must be periodically rechecked and intricate electronic equipment kept in perfect working order, with radar scope adjustments refined to precision settings. Steering information, radio transmission and reception, exhaust temperatures, and fuel and hydraulic pressures must all be within exact tolerances to allow the aircrew a chance for a splash kill. Three of every four men with the 54th are on the ground, working to keep the F-89J Scorpions combat ready. Maintenance is of such quality that during the recent firepower demonstration, all 27 planes by the 54th were able to fly any time they were scheduled without malfunctions, cancellations, or late take-offs.[54]

The 54th FIS also received the following award and description in 1958:

Central Air Defense Force "A" Award. Under the provisions of paragraph 23a(1), Air Defense Command Manual 51-2, dated December 1, 1958, the Central Air Defense Force "A" Award is awarded to the following named organization for meritorious achievement during the period indicated: 54th Fighter-Interceptor Squadron, November 1, 1958, to December 31, 1958.[55]

The 54th Fighter-Interceptor Squadron has distinguished itself as an outstanding air defense unit from 1 November through December 31, 1958. During this period they were highly successful in a Central Air Defense Force tactical evaluation exercise and showed outstanding command operational readiness inspection. Early in 1958, this unit completed a complex aircraft conversion program and resumed its full operational commitments in a very short time. Both operational and engineering effectiveness rapidly improved throughout the year, and on December 16–17, 1958, this superlative performance was climaxed by setting an all-time high record of achievement at Vincent AFB Weapons Center.[56]

For the 54th FIS, its organization and operations were specified by Headquarters 29th Air Division (Defense), "Organization-Field, Organization and Function's Fighter-Interceptor Squadrons," 29AD Manual, No. 23-1, Malmstrom AFB, Montana, dated June 1, 1959:

Chapter I
Section I
Introduction

1. The ranges of modern military aircraft have been developed to the point where no longer is any nation secure from air attack by reason of distance alone. Coincident with the development of the means for intercontinental ranges in large-scale operations, revolutionary progress has been made in increasing the effectiveness of mass destruction weapons, which are deliverable from the air.
2. For a nation such as the United States, having a highly organized industrialized society and great population center and vital defense bases, the implications in sudden air attack are critical and the absolute need for highly effective and constantly ready defenses is immediately apparent.

3. Continuous strides are being made in the development of improved defense weapons. These become increasingly more complex and costly. To obtain maximum benefit from these new devices, we must achieve maximum efficiency in our operations. This can be done by planning, proper indoctrination and training, effective utilization of our resources, retention of our technical competence, and standardization. This manual is a step toward improving standardization and outlining functions and responsibilities within the organizational structure.

Chapter I
Section III, Mission
Fighter-Interceptor Squadron

The primary mission of a fighter-interceptor squadron is to achieve and maintain a level of operational effectiveness which will enable a squadron to intercept, identify and/or destroy airborne weapons under all conditions of weather during daylight and darkness. [This is what the 54th FIS was tasked to accomplish at Ellsworth AFB, responding to identify airborne threats armed with conventional AAMs. If an increased DECON was authorized due to an external threat from the Soviet Union, the 54th FIS F-89Js could be armed with nuclear warhead tipped Genie AAMs.]

Chapter II
The Command Element
Section I
The Squadron Commander

1. Function. The Commander of a Fighter-Interceptor Squadron is responsible for exercising command over all personnel in the organization. His overall direction, guidance, and coordination of the various activities insures the accomplishment of the squadron mission.

2. Responsibilities.
a. The Commander must plan, review and direct the organization activities, insure maintenance of the highest operational effectiveness. He must maintain close contact with branch chiefs and make periodic visits to, and inspections of squadron activities in order to gain first-hand knowledge of the overall situation and to provide guidance and direction where necessary.
b. He must support the maintenance effort by quality accomplishment of maintenance responsibilities in accordance with applicable maintenance plans and policies. Advise his Maintenance Officer(s) of his policies and the requirements and permit the Maintenance Officer(s) to manage the maintenance activity within those established guidelines. Necessary authority must be delegated to the Maintenance Officer(s) to accomplish duties. In

line with this, the Commander must insure maximum availability of maintenance personnel for duty and to prevent disruption of maintenance schedules. He must review and indorse all quality inspection reports concerning his maintenance activities and insure necessary action to correct deficient areas promptly.
c. Establishes organizational policies, procedures and coordinates the overall squadron effort to insure timely and efficient achievement of operational and training commitments.
d. Provides for the morale and welfare of assigned personnel.
e. Provides guidance and direction to contract technical representatives on duty with the squadron. These personnel work very closely with the Maintenance Officer(s) in resolving maintenance problems and conduct training.
f. The Commander is assisted in his administrative responsibilities by the Executive Officer.
g. Responsible for establishing a Flight Scheduling Committee on special orders. Appropriate branch chiefs to serve on this committee. In a CAMRON under group/base concept, this is a responsibility of the Group Commander.

3. General narrative.
a. The Squadron Commander is in all matters responsible to higher headquarters; however, because of the complexity and scope of modern day fighter-interceptor squadrons, necessary authority must be delegated to the various branch chiefs to manage their elements of the squadron. It is extremely important to the combat effectiveness of the organization that the Commander establish and maintain a close relationship with his various branch chiefs. The Commander must insure that proper coordination is maintained among the branch chiefs and that they fully understand their responsibilities.
b. The Commander must continually review his organization to insure proper balance between personnel capability, maintenance capability and operational requirement are maintained. An improperly balanced condition will gradually and surely result in a loss in squadron effectiveness. Organizational balance which may be destroyed by improper manning, excessive amounts of untrained personnel, undue emphasis placed upon one organizational element, excessive requirements placed upon operations or maintenance or lack of proper supervision and guidance; therefore, the Commander must be alert to avoid these conditions.
c. The demands upon the Commander's time and personnel attention are extremely heavy. In addition to regular staff meetings and inspections he must devote a considerable amount of personal attention to administrative details and duties. He engages in frequent crew training activities to maintain his proficiency. There are personal interviews, civic and base responsibilities and visits to and from higher headquarters; therefore, the utmost efficiency

must be practiced by the Commander in scheduling his activities and in the delegation of duties and commensurate authority to his subordinates. The need for sound application of the principles of organization and management are essential.

Chapter II
Section II
The Executive Officer

1. Function. The Executive Officer supervises the overall administrative functions of the squadron.

2. Responsibilities: The Executive Officer.
a. Assists the Commander in overall supervision and is responsible for administrative functions of the squadron. Establishes procedures for operating and maintaining files, suspense systems and security registry systems. Insures proper dissemination of information to all branches.
b. Makes studies of organizational and manning requirements of the unit and submits commendations. Also, surveys procedures and facilities and makes recommendations for improvements.
c. Appoints boards and committees and monitors their activities.
d. Supervises the operation of the Alert Mess.

3. General narrative.
a. The Executive Officer us an individual in whom the Commander must shoulder the majority of the administrative work load to free the commander for more time to devote to the overall direction of the squadron. The Executive Officer, in conjunction with the First Sergeant, must accomplish this, and these individuals can be largely responsible for a smoothly functioning unit.
b. The Executive Officer should be a senior and mature individual with considerable experience in administrative and personnel procedures and policies. Since all correspondence, reports, etc., pass across his desk, he is in the best position to keep the commander informed of conditions and trends within the organization. He closely supervises the operation of the Unit Administration Branch.
c. He is responsible for monitoring the accurate and timely submission of the numerous reports required of a squadron. He coordinates with, and provides guidance to the branch chiefs on matters relating to administration, reporting, preparation of correspondence, suspense dates, etc.
d. The Executive Officer prepares regular and special staff meetings conducted by the Commander by insuring that the necessary personnel are at the

appointed place at the proper time. Minutes or policies emanating from these meetings are normally prepared by him or under his supervision.

Chapter I
Section III

Section of the 54th FIS aircraft parts maintenance hangar. *South Dakota Air and Space Museum Archives*

Flight Scheduling Committee Meetings

1. Function. To provide a maximum operation capability and provide optimum workload for aircraft maintenance organization.

2. Responsibilities.
a. The Group or Squadron Commander will appoint an Aircraft Scheduling Committee on special orders. This committee will determine the productive capability of the maintenance organization and develop a flying schedule providing the maximum operational mission commensurate with this capacity. This committee will consist of, but not be limited to the following personnel:

(1) Group or Squadron Commander.
(2) Group or Squadron Operations/Training Officer.

(3) Chief of Maintenance.
   (4) Maintenance Control Officer.
   (5) Base Supply Officer or his representative.

b. The Flight Scheduling Committee will meet monthly as directed by the Commander.
c. A weekly Flight Scheduling Sub-committee will be formed to discuss weekly problems encountered. This weekly meeting need consist only of Chief of Maintenance, Maintenance Control Officer, Director of Operations (if it is applicable), and Operations Officers.
d. The monthly maintenance plan and the monthly flight schedule will be furnished to all agencies concerned.

3. General narrative.
a. There are certain governing or limiting factors that must be considered when determining maintenance capability. These are:

   (1) The number of aircraft made available for operational use will not exceed 80 percent of the possessed primary mission aircraft for the alert and training commitments. Although this applies to training exercises, it does not refer to NORAD or ADC directed exercises.
   (2) Average minimum length of time required to perform the inspection, maintenance and/or repair which become necessary at the end of a sortie.
   (3) The number of aircraft an organization is capable of turning around in a given time.
   (4) Equipment and tool limitations.

b. The capability of the maintenance organization to produce the required flying hours and number of sorties should be determined before attempting any operational program. This will prevent over-scheduling with the resultant loss in combat readiness and, likewise, under scheduling with the resultant loss of training hours. With such balance, it is possible to increase overall effectiveness of the maintenance organization while, at the same time, increasing the productive capability of individual activities.

The 54th Fighter-Interceptor Squadron

Commander Lt. Col. Ernest B. Nuckols Jr. outside the 54th FIS Headquarters and Administrative building (October 1959) after the squadron won the Hughes Award. *Courtesy Master Sgt. Robert O'Daniel*

Chapter III
Unit Administrative Branch
Section I
The Administrative Branch Officer

1. Function. The Administrative Officer is the Chief of the Administrative Branch and is directly responsible to the Executive Officer for the operation of the personnel and administration function.

2. Responsibilities. The Administrative Officer.
a. Manages and directs administrative services activities.
b. Establishes administrative policies and procedures. Coordinates with other branch chiefs or administrative matters and procedures, personnel assignment, training, or reassignment of personnel. Publishes and distributes orders, along with directives, official correspondence and other communications. Maintains unit records and files.
c. Coordinates with the Executive Officer in determining organizational requirements by analyzing assigned mission, skill qualification necessary and interpreting directives, orders and regulations.

d. Evaluates requirements, establishes controls and stock levels to provide adequate stocks of publications and blank forms.
   e. Manages separation, re-enlistment and career guidance counseling.

3. General narrative.
a. An effective administration and personnel program is vital to a smoothly operating organization. A great deal of time and effort is required to manage the activities of the Administrative Branch. Continuous checks are necessary to insure proper and expeditious routing of correspondence, that suspense dates are met, that personnel records are properly maintained, and that all activities relating to promotions, training, assignment and reassignment are being accomplished.
b. The Administrative Officer is a combination of Administrative Officer and Personnel Officer. In the administrative services area, he supervises the activities of publications, reproduction and distribution. He supervises personnel in the identification of records material suitable for historical purposes, determines records disposition schedules and procedures. In the personnel area, he is required to monitor personnel activities such as assignments, classifications, effectiveness ratings, and job and organizational analyses. His branch maintains military personnel records and provides counseling on personal affairs matters, separations, re-enlistment, financial services, etc.

4. The First Sergeant.
a. Even though the First Sergeant is authorized in this function, he works with and for the executive officer and has access to the Commander at all times. The first sergeant has a prime interest in maintaining unit discipline, morale, the orderliness, welfare, and in the general appearance and condition of the squadron personnel, area and living conditions. He advises incoming personnel on squadron policies, work schedules, base facilities, restricted areas, etc. He performs a very important function in counseling of airmen on personnel matters.
b. In accordance with the Commander's policies, he informs personnel of schedules for inspections, military training, recreational and housekeeping facilities. He accompanies the inspecting officer on all inspections. He assembles personnel for formations, drills, ceremonies, etc., and arranges for unit recreation, entertainment, facilities and sports activities.
c. The First Sergeant must be a good military leader as well as an administrative manager. As he is required to deal with all ranks of airmen, he must retain both their respect and confidence. He is the liaison contact between the Commander and the airman.

Chapter III
Section II
The Administrative Section

1. Function. Prepares correspondence, maintains files and performs related clerical duties.

2. Responsibilities. The Administrative Section.
a. Receives, prepares, dispatches, distributes and files incoming and outgoing correspondence. Maintains logging filing, control and suspense systems.
b. Maintains central reference library of publications and directives.
c. Consolidates, complies and forwards requests for technical publications, manuals, regulations and office supplies.
d. Performs unit mail and distribution activities.

3. General narrative.
a. Personnel of this section must be reliable, efficient and skilled because this section can have a direct effect upon the operation of the entire squadron. Correspondence must be accurately and expeditiously routed, directives and publications must be supplied to the users, reports must be submitted on time, and suspense systems must be maintained. The proper maintenance, indexing, controlling, accounting and disposition of files and records is a very important function. The preparation of annual records disposition schedules and selection of records for disposition, retirement, or historical material requires judgment, careful management, and attention.
b. As in other sections, work within this section is sectionalized, the degree which is independent upon the manning. Control of correspondence, publications, and overall direction of the section are responsibilities of the section chief. The typist prepares correspondence, reports, requests, etc. The file clerk is primarily responsible for maintenance of various files. However, as the work load and situation dictates, each will have to assist the other.

Chapter III
Section III
The Personnel Section

1. Function. Maintains personnel records and reports and provides personnel counseling, classification and guidance.

2. Responsibilities. The Personnel Section.
a. Conducts interviews of personnel and advises on personal affairs, insurance, bonds, allotments, Veteran's benefits, separation and re-enlistments. Explains to personnel sources and/or benefits of such facilities as Air Force Aid Society, Red Cross, Chaplain, Judge Advocate and Soldiers 7 Sailors Relief Act.

b. Insures compliance with records maintenance procedures established by higher headquarters. In conjunction with this, direct the activities of the records units. Insures records of incoming and departing personnel are current, accurate and in compliance with current directives.

3. General narrative.
a. The activities of this section are of vital concern to each individual of the squadron. The records maintained have a permanent and guiding effect upon the career of each individual. Because of this, the need for accuracy and completeness of the information inserted in these records cannot be over-emphasized.
b. Personal affairs counseling is an extremely important service that should be readily available to all personnel. The directives concerning such matters are complex and subject to frequent changes; and they are not easily understood by the majority. The Personnel Section must have the capability to counsel personnel in these matters or be able to direct inquiries to the proper sources.

Chapter III
Section IV
The On-The-Job-Training (OJT) Section

1. Function. Supervises the OJT program for all personnel of the squadron with the exception of those assigned to the Maintenance Branch OJT for these personnel will be supervised by the Standardization, Training and CTSP Section.

2. Responsibilities. OJT Section.
a. Maintains the squadron OJT program and assists supervisory personnel in the conduct of OJT for their personnel.
b. Procures and distributes OJT package programs, training materials, necessary forms and directives.
c. Screens records of incoming personnel to determine their need and eligibility for OJT.
d. Coordinates with the Base Training Officer, Base I & E Officer and the Squadron Maintenance Officer.

3. General narrative.
a. The Squadron Manning Document will not normally reflect any authorization for this section. Consequently, the functions of this section will be performed by additional duty personnel.
b. It is the duty of the OJT Supervisor and his assistant to assist the supervisory personnel of the other offices of the organization in conducting the OJT program. They will do this by providing guidance, insuring compliance with applicable directives and proper preparation for those who complete training.

c. The OJT Section and the Training Unit of the Maintenance Branch will coordinate closely to insure all personnel eligible for OJT are receiving OJT as prescribed in current, applicable directives.

Chapter IV
Alert Mess

1. Function. Provides mess of alert flight crews and ground support personnel 24 hours per day, seven days per week.

2. Responsibilities. The Alert Mess.
a. Maintains proper standards of food preparation, cleanliness and food preparation.
b. Requests, receives and stores food stuffs and supplies.
c. Maintains appropriate records and accounts for funds as prescribed by applicable directives.

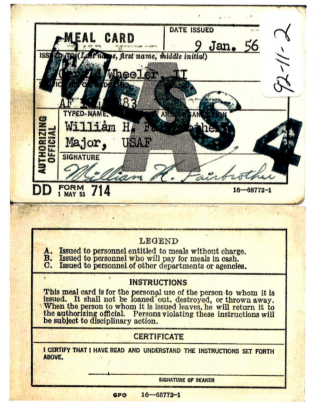

An alert meal card of Maj. William H. Fairbrother, former 54th FIS commander, dated 9 January 1956. *Courtesy Master Sgt. Robert O'Daniel*

3. General narrative.
   The Alert Mess operates under the supervision of the Executive Officer and is maintained primarily for the Alert Flight and ground crews who must remain in the vicinity of the flight line and prepare for immediate scramble.

Chapter V
The Operations Branch
Section I
The Operations Branch Officer

1. Function. Monitors and directs aircrew programs and activities to attain the highest degree of combat readiness.

2. Responsibilities. The Operations Officer.
   a. Is responsible to the Commander for accomplishment of the flying training and operational programs. In conjunction with this, he insures each flight accomplishes its equitable share of the training commitment.
   b. Insures implementation of training and operational directives from higher headquarters. Prepares plans, SOPs and directives pertaining to aircrew training, operations, flying safety and emergency situations.
   c. Participates in weekly flight scheduling meetings and briefs, or supervises the briefing of aircrews.
   d. Insures accurate and complex flights records are maintained for all assigned aircrew personnel.
   e. Establishes and maintains close coordination with the Maintenance Officer and his sections.

3. General narrative.
   a. It is the job of the operations officer, under the direction of the commander, to fulfill the mission of the squadron by insuring that the aircrews, the aircraft and the weapons systems are molded into an efficient and effective air arm. Personnel has supplied the people. Maintenance has supplied the serviceable aircraft and weapons; but these efforts are worthless if they are not employed against the target at the proper time and in the most efficient manner.
   b. The operations officer must closely supervise aircrew training activities to insure that they are conducted to provide combat ready crews in the shortest possible time. He must be alert for symptoms or trends, which indicate approaching hazardous situations and take corrective actions. Any changes in operational procedures or techniques must be understood by the aircrews.
   c. Another important function of the Operations Officer is in the supervision of flight records maintenance. These records provide the basis for flight pay, accomplishment of annual requirements, skill upgrading, awards and decorations. They must be current and properly and accurately maintained.

d. The operations officer supervises the operation of the personal equipment, insuring that crews are provided with proper functioning personal equipment. From time-to-time, qualified personnel from the Personal Equipment Section will be required to instruct aircrews in the proper use and care of personal equipment.

e. Personal Equipment Section. For fighter- interceptor squadrons which are located on an ADC base, or under the command of a fighter- interceptor group, this function will be performed by the supporting Air Base Group or Squadron, and whichever is appropriate. Those fighter-interceptor squadrons which are tenants on bases of other commands will have this section organized as per the organization chart.

Chapter V
Section III
Flights

1. Function. To achieve and maintain, under leadership of the Flight Commander, readiness of aircrews leading to interception and/or destruction of directed aerial targets.

2. Responsibilities.

a. Flight Commanders plan, schedule and direct activities of their assigned aircrews. In addition, they will evaluate policies, procedures and requirements relating to flight operations and aircrews, and make appropriate recommendations to the Operations Officer.

b. Flights will perform scheduled and unscheduled training, directed missions and scramble alert.

3. General narrative.

a. The number of flights in a squadron will vary depending upon aircraft assigned, crew-to-aircraft ratios, alert commitments, etc. Normally, there are five flights of which one may be a training flight.

b. The Flight Commander is in the best position to determine the capabilities of aircrews since it is he who works with them on a day-to-day basis and observes their performance. It is his function to select the best qualified for instructors, flight tests, advancement, etc., and to concentrate training on lesser qualified crews.

Chapter V
Section III
Squadron Radar Observer

1. Function. Advises the Operations Officer and the Commander on all matters pertaining to airborne radar and Radar Observers.

2. Responsibilities.
a. Advises the Commander on matters relating to proficiencies of, and training requirements for, unit radar observers and on matters pertaining to operation, techniques and performances of aircraft radar intercept equipment.
b. Instructs radar observers in the operation of equipment, techniques, and uses of NADAR and scope recordings for critiques, instruction and grading.
c. Conducts training and checks to insure that highest standards of proficiency are maintained among radar observers.

3. General narrative.
a. The Squadron Radar Observer, while not authorized as such, normally fills a crew space authorization and his selection is based upon experience, knowledge and ability to advise, instruct and train.
b. The Commander must rely considerably upon the Squadron Radar Observer to correctly judge the proficiencies of crews and limitations of equipment to assist in devising ways and means of maintaining maximum proficiency of crews.
c. The Squadron Radar Observer must coordinate closely with armament. Electronics maintenance crews in the maintenance and repair of airborne radar and associated equipment.

Chapter V
Section IV
Air Operations Section

1. Function. Maintains personnel flight records, air operations and alert dispatch facilities.

2. Responsibilities.
a. The Air Operations Supervisor is responsible to the operations officer for supervision of the Flight Records Unit and the Alert Unit. This person insures proper maintenance of flight records, issuance of flight orders and preparation of reports, correspondence and files. In addition, this section maintains current flight information, charts, maps and information for the flight aircrews.
b. Advises Operations Officer on clearing, scheduling, dispatching of aircraft, setting up crews, etc.
c. The Alert Unit receives scramble notices and notifies alert crews and Operations.

3. General narrative.
a. The Air Operations Section and its units perform administrative services for the Operations Officer and provides a records keeping for all rated members of the squadron. The Alert Unit is the link between the Air Defense

Direction Center and the alert crews. This unit receives scramble notices from the Direction Center and passes the information to alert aircrews, ground crews and the tower.

b. The Air Operations Section must maintain current directives and procedures for the benefit of flight crews. Up-to-date information on routes, restricted areas, safety areas, etc., must be maintained. The Air Operations Section must assure that only current information is displayed and that changes are posted upon receipt.

Chapter V
Section V
Personal Equipment Section

1. Function. Provides aircrews with properly functioning and fitted personal equipment and training in the use of equipment.

2. Responsibilities.
a. Issues, fits and/or personal equipment such as parachutes, life vests, survival gear, oxygen masks and related gear, and special items of flight equipment. Also services, clean, lubricates and performs minor maintenance on this equipment.
b. Receives and stores personal equipment. Determines stock levels and requirements and submits requisitions. Accomplishes those technical order compliances that are within capabilities.
c. Instructs aircrews in survival training and use and care of personal equipment.

3. General narrative.
a. The Personal Equipment Section has a very important function in insuring that all aircrews are properly fitted with functioning equipment and understand its use and limitations. This section provides another service by lecturing, instructing and demonstrating the use of individual items of equipment.
b. This function will be provided by the supporting Air Base Group or Squadron for those fighter-interceptor squadrons located on an ADC base or under the command of a fighter-interceptor group.

Chapter VI
The Maintenance Branch
Section I

1. Functions. The responsibilities, organization structure and operational instructions for the Maintenance Branch are contained in ADC Manual 66-2. These subjects are explained in detail in referenced manual and no changes will be made without prior approval of this headquarters.[57]

A 54th FIS maintenance hangar. At the date of this photograph the squadron was still equipped with the F-86D. *Courtesy Master Sgt. Robert O'Daniel*

1959

The official history of the 54th FIS for January–April 1, 1959, states:

> The squadron has continued to maintain the high standards it posted during the deployment to the ADC weapons training program at Vincent AFB in December 1958. The squadron has participated in numerous 29th Air Division exercises, maintained aircrew proficiency through radar training missions, and also initiated cross-training with AC&W sites in its area.
>
> The squadron has worked to maintain a high degree of proficiency in its aircrews' effectiveness through daily radar training missions whenever possible. These were against SAC B-52 Stratofortresses. The Electronic Warfare Officer (EWO) was stationed in a small cubical size space at the right hand aft extremity of the upper deck. The EWO had a full range of defensive electronics to protect the aircraft from attacking fighters: ALQ-155 EW power management system, ALQ-122 Smart Noise Operation Equipment false target generator, ALQ-117 tail mounted deception jammer for use against radar-guided air-to-air missiles, such as those carried by the F-89J and ALQ-153 tail warning system, plus active tail mounted four .50-caliber machine guns to defend against an

enemy fighter that might attempt to close in on the rear of the B-52. The EWO performed ECM as what would be encountered from penetrating Russian Air Force bombers. It was excellent training for F-89J squadrons, as well as SAC bomber crews.

A conscious effort has been made to coordinate these missions with the various AC&W sites so it will be possible for the two to work closely together in close harmony. A schedule has been established so that each site is assured of a minimum of live intercepts per week.

	Jan	Feb	March	Total
Profiles attempted	143	157	178	478
Profiles successful	121	144	165	430
Percent made	84	94	94	90[58]

A program of cross-training between the squadron and AC&W sites in the local area were incepted during this reporting period. Once a month, three-man teams from the squadron have visited the various high-line sites for three-day periods to observe and work with the GCI personnel. The crew members have had an opportunity to work closely with the sites and come to a better understanding of their mission. They have also been able to make them aware of the problem noted by ADC inspection teams. On the other hand, directors from AC&W sites have visited the squadron at Ellsworth AFB to observe the squadron's operations and make suggestions for increased efficiency and closer harmony.

The 54th FIS also participated in several 29th AD training exercises during this reporting period, and demonstrated its ability to maintain a high level of combat proficiency.

Date of profile	Success rate	Intercept Success
8 January	76 percent	61 percent
21 January	50 percent	54 percent
29 January	80 percent	71 percent
6 February	90 percent	91 percent
26 February	90 percent	87 percent
12 March	82 percent	71 percent
23 March	94 percent	91 percent
26 March	89 percent	86 percent[59]

February: Maj. James C. Brown arrived as new Executive Officer.
10 March: Maj. Robert W. Gibson replaced Capt. William Norris as Operations Officer.
7–22 March: Two Air Force Academy students, Gordon S. Savage Jr. and Kerry D. Miller, spend a training tour with the squadron.

A 54th Fighter-Interceptor Squadron press release, "54th FIS host to Air Force Academy Third Lieutenants," Ellsworth AFB, South Dakota, March 24, 1959, notes:

> From March 7–22, 1959, the 54th Fighter-Interceptor Squadron entertained "Operation Third Lieutenant" when Air Force Academy Second Classman Gordon S. Savage Jr. and Kerry D. Miller arrived at Ellsworth AFB for a three week training tour. During their stay, the two Air Force Academy cadets actively participated in the everyday work activities of the squadron, studying first hand the leadership and management techniques employed in command and staff work. Cadet Savage, assigned to the Operations Scheduling Section, worked in close harmony with Captain Eugene D. Levy, 54th Operations Officer, solving the pre-briefing problems of aircraft determination, aircrew scheduling, and coordination with approach control and the mission GCI sites. In addition, he assisted the NADAR section in assessing the mission film to determine the percentages of practice "kills" or misses. Cadet Miller, for his part, was assigned to the Armament Section of the 54th under Major James L. Brewer, where he assisted in the correction and revision of existing maintenance control reorganization procedures. Both Air Force Academy undergraduates were trained through actual practice in the deadly skilled profession of running live intercepts or alleged enemy aircraft simulating penetration of the national borders. Interception flights and ground school were combined to make this lesson more effective. Both cadets emphatically attested to the value of this unique program designed to develop in the cadet as a person first hand understanding of the leadership problems confronting an Air Force officer in a top, front line, combat ready organization. The 54th FIS and Ellsworth AFB join in extending a welcome to the two cadets and profess sincere enthusiasm and delight in being a part of this program to improve the future development of Air Force leadership.

15 May: Lt. Col. Flake departed for a new assignment. Maj. Brown assumed command until the arrival of Lt. Col. Ernest B. Nuckols Jr.

May: The 54th FIS lost a shoot-off for representation at the William Tell meet to the 29th FIS due to malfunction of an RME.

2 June: Five aircrews gave a flyover to the first graduating class at the Air Force Academy.[60]

The historical record provides the following description of events around this time:

> From 2 through 4 June, the largest and most complex target force ever used for a Central Air Defense Force Tactical Evaluation was sent against the 54th FIS. In addition, hard evasive action, ECM, and T-33s flying at

altitudes of 1,000 feet above the terrain used in an effort to saturate the 54th FIS defensive area of responsibility as what might be expected from an attempt by Russian bombers to scatter and penetrate to their individual targets at low level. All such efforts were unsuccessful, despite an acute shortage of aircrew personnel.

Deployment of 54th FIS F-89Js to Minot AFB was outstandingly successful in neutralizing most of the target force, ranging far into Canada and often hitting the striker aircraft within seconds of their initial point. [The ADC wanted to intercept Russian Air Force bombers as far north as possible to prevent any release of nuclear weapons in the United States.] It was necessary to impose simulated minimums on weather at Minot AFB and the second day of the exercise to generate desired activity at Ellsworth AFB.

Air discipline for the exercise was declared outstanding: during the two days 82 sorties were flown, 91 intercepts attempted (80 were charged to the 54th FIS), and 72 recorded for a success rate of 90 percent. There were three ground aborts charged to the squadron. Of the 19 missed intercepts, four were due to airborne equipment failure, four to personnel error, and 11 to the GCI sites.

The most serious problem facing squadron operations was the rapid turnover of experienced aircrew personnel. Date of separation personnel and transfers were the main causes for the crippling turnover. There has been a shortage of radar observers over the last few months, with many leaving and no new ones assigned to alleviate the manpower problem. Flying time for radar missions averaged approximately 700 hours per month for this period. However, the amount which is needed for the essential radar training has been cut by the squadron's being required to furnish many targets for Air Division attached personnel.[61]

21 July: Lt. Col. Ernest B. Nuckols Jr. assumed command.
28 July: Practice mass loading of aircraft.[62]

The 54th FIS' engineering department noted the following:

Led by Squadron Commander Lt. Col. Alma Ross Flake, the 54th FIS from Ellsworth AFB, South Dakota, shattered 28 individual records in nation-wide ADC competition during an exhaustive 21-day exercise conducted at the National Air Defense Command Rocket Range at Vincent Air Force Base, Yuma, Arizona. The spectacular performance by the 54th, flying F-89J Scorpions carrying Hughes MG-12 Radar Fire Control systems, earned unstinted praise.

Col. Benjamin H. King, Wing Commander of the evaluating 4750th Air Defense Wing: "The 54th FIS has been by far the finest F-89J squadron that has come through this station, and as far as that's concerned, the finest of any type unit that has been to Yuma."

Lt. Col. Alma R. Flake (right), commander, 54th Fighter-Interceptor Squadron, and Capt. L. Melton Jr. (left), squadron radar observer, on the wing of their F-89J after returning from one of the successful missions during the squadron's 21-day exercise conducted at the National Air Defense Command Rocket Range, Vincent AFB, Arizona. The 54th FIS broke the existing all-time global Air Defense Command records during this meet.
Courtesy Master Sgt. Robert O'Daniel

Major William R. Williamson, Evaluator and Director of Operations, 4750th Air Defense Wing: "Why bother to count them? [records]. You've broken every record we've got here."

Here's what the 54th did.

For the first time in the two years the range has been in operation, there was not a single firing pass missed in the tactical evaluation phase due to a radar fire control fire control system malfunction, an aircraft malfunction, a radio, NADAR, or camera malfunction.

In addition, the 54th Maintenance and Radar personnel maintained an operational combat-ready aircraft status through the entire Yuma stay, which far exceeded that of the closest competitor. And all 27 competing aircraft flew both days of the tactical evaluation exercise, a tribute to Armament Assembly personnel.

As a result of the efforts of the MG-12 FCS and maintenance personnel, aircrews were able to set 17 records of their own.

Besides compiling the highest competition score ever recorded during an ADC tactical evaluation exercise, they also managed to set, among others, new records, for the first day's firing, for the first week's firing, and for the entire "dry" phase firing portion. While actual figures are classified [at that time], the results are little short of incredible, Air Force sources reported.

Lt. Col. J.L. Nollkamper, Director of Operations and Training, 29th Air Division: "As long as human beings control machines and machines are fallible, I believe this almost 100 percent success rate and team record will remain unsurpassed. This squadron had just rewritten and proved the ADC doctrine."

Evaluations were made on every phase of the mission, from the assembly and loading of the weapons, to the scramble procedure, and finally to the sharp shooting techniques of the aircrews who fired every six minutes into predetermined firing cone missile range at high speed target towed 13,000 feet behind a Canberra jet bomber.

D.L. Hopkins, HAC Field Engineer, 54th FIS: "Brilliantly coordinated efforts of maintenance personnel, aircraft control and warning intercept controllers, and aircrews resulted in the overall team victory. While no one of these units can take more credit than the rest, special commendation must go to the radar and maintenance crews who by literally working around the clock, seven days a week, brought the aircraft and their associated fire control systems to a state of excellent unsurpassed in memory of any of the operational personnel."

He also praised Lt. Col. Flake for infusing the entire squadron with the confidence and desire for: "That extra effort which so often spells the difference between victory and being an also-ran in tough competition."[63]

Another document summarized the competition:

The 54th, led by Lt. Col. Alma Ross Flake, competed against 47 other ADC squadrons at the National Air Defense Command Rocket Range at Vincent Air Force Base, Yuma, Arizona. Equipped with 27 missile launchings, twin-jet Northrop F-89J Scorpions, 32 crack aircrews, plus a 203 man contingent maintenance group were deployed to the Yuma Range for the annual firepower test.[64]

History of the 54th FIS

Smiles on the members of Ellsworth AFB's 54th Fighter-Interceptor squadron prior to their trip to Miami, Florida, to attend the Air Force Association's convention, where they will be awarded the Hughes Trophy, an award for outstanding performance (from left to right): Lt. Col. Ernest B. Nuckols Jr., 54th FIS commander; Maj. William R. Blackburn, 740th ACW operations officer; Tech. Sgt. Charles E. Tipton, NCOIC Fire Control Section; Capt. Joseph H. Pertl Jr., operations officer; Capt. Leonard L. Melton Jr., squadron radar observer; and (bottom of aircraft ladder) Donald L. Hopkins, senior field engineer, Hughes Aircraft Company. Also attending was Senior Master Sgt. J. M. Mortensen, NCOIC Maintenance Control Section. Lt. Col. Alma Flake was reassigned during the exercise. *Courtesy Master Sgt. Robert O'Daniel*

The *Rapid City Journal* wrote about the 54th FIS achieving the Hughes Trophy:

The 54th Fighter-Interceptor Squadron at Ellsworth AFB has won the Hughes Trophy, symbolic of air defense supremacy. Given annually, the award salutes the outstanding operational fighter-interceptor squadron as selected by the Air Force Tactical Evaluation Team from nominees in Eastern, Western, and Central Air Defense Forces, as well as the European, Pacific, Far East, Caribbean, and Alaskan Commands. A six man delegation

95

from the 54th will go to Miami, Florida, scene of the Air Force Association convention, to accept the award at the Night Fighters Association banquet on 4 September. Making the trip will be Lt. Col. Ernest B. Nuckols Jr., new squadron commander; Major William R. Blackburn, Operations Officer of the 740th A&W Squadron; Captain Joseph H. Pertl, Jr., Assistant 54th Operations Officer; Captain Leonard Melton, Squadron Radar Observer; MSgt. Jay M. Mortensen, Non-Commissioned Officer in Charge of the 54th Maintenance Control Section; and TSgt. Charles Tipton, Non-Commissioned officer in Charge of the 54th Fire Control Section to accept the award at the Night Fighters Association on 4 September. Accompanying the group will be Brigadier General Harold Heely, 29th Air Division Commander, and Donald L. Hopkins, Senior Field Engineer for Hughes Aircraft Company, who is serving as a Technical Representative with the 54th. The Hughes Trophy, symbol of the award and permanent possession of the squadron, is a giant bowl shaped trophy, standing 20-inches high on its base and measuring two feet in diameter. It is designed in silver and lined with gold.

Julian Focan, Hughes employee and Belgium silversmith, spent a year creating the original Hughes Trophy. In a Union Telegram from Focan to Lt. Col. Nuckols:

Dear Colonel: At this time I wish to congratulate you and all of the men connected with the 54th FIS for having won the Hughes Achievement Award. Please convey my regrets for not being present. I am very proud to have had a small part in the executing of this great award. Like General Lawrence S. Kuter stated in Miami, you are champions among the professionals.

The Air Force award is made on the basis of an elaborate point system devised to test and probe squadron efficiency in rocketry or missile qualification (40 percent); profile mission daily success rate (92.5 percent); aircraft maintenance and percent of operational-ready aircraft (25 percent); and aircraft flying safety records (10 percent).[65]

The *Rapid City Journal* detailed the Hughes Trophy acceptance in the following article:

Tired, but proud and happy, the seven-man 54th Fighter-Interceptor Squadron Miami "Team" returned from their week-long stay at the United States Air Force Aerospace Panorama, bringing with them the 1959 Hughes Achievement Award and the coveted title of "World Champion of Air Defense." The Miami Beach meeting, the largest Air Force-industry showcase in the world, was attended by 4,000 high-ranking leaders from all walks of life, including Secretary of the Air Force James H. Douglas and Air Force Chief of Staff General Thomas D. White. Before this distinguished gathering, the 54th FIS of Rapid City was described as "officially the best of the best."

Members of the 54th FIS in front of the Hughes Trophy Award at the Air Force Association's convention (left to right): Capt. Leonard L. Melton Jr., Donald L. Hopkins, Lt. Col. Ernest B. Nuckols Jr., Gen. Lawrence S. Kuter, Maj. William R. Blackburn, and Capt. Joseph H. Pertl Jr. Kneeling (left to right) are Tech. Sgt. Charles E. Tipton and Senior Master Sgt. J.M. Mortensen. *Courtesy Master Sgt. Robert O'Daniel.*

The speakers' schedule appeared as an Air Force Who's Who. The 54th FIS award, presented by the new Commander-in-Chief of the North American Defense Command, four-star General Lawrence S. Kuter, who was the first made at the annual Night-Fighter Association banquet. The "Team" and the trophy were introduced again at General White's Aerospace banquet in the Grand Ballroom of the Hotel Fontainebleau at the high point of the week long convention. Here, through the 54th FIS, the name of Ellsworth AFB and the outstanding role it plays, was carried before attending Air Force leaders such as General Curtis E. LeMay, Vice Chief of Staff, USAF, and General Thomas S. Power, Commander-in-Chief, Strategic Air Command.

General Kuter, in making the presentation, called the 54th fighter outfit: "The outstanding squadron among the pros."

His only note of regret was that the entire squadron could not be present to share in the plaudits, but that as an: "alert battle-worthy fighter organization, the rest were back at Ellsworth doing what fighter squadrons are supposed to be doing."

The 54th FIS success story will be told and retold time after time. From relative obscurity the "working airman" of the group emerged successfully from a competition which evaluated every facet of intercept capability: operational readiness, proficiency in firing, maintenance, safety and training effectiveness. The crowning achievement till now was, of course, the 28 world records set by the Air Force Weapons Test Center.

The high caliber of air defense squadrons throughout the world makes finishing on top a difficult task. The selection process itself, where the Air Force's Tactical Evaluation Team reviews thousands of intercept profile missions, is a complicated process. Therefore, it is with a tremendous sense of satisfaction and pride that the 54th Fighter-Interceptor Squadron can accept the $25,000 trophy knowing that it represents a symbol of what 506 men can do working toward a common goal, the development of a striking force determined to protect the ideal of a free world enmeshed in a desire of eventual peace. The $25,000 Hughes Achievement Award Trophy stands 20-inches high on its base, measures 24-inches in diameter, and holds 9.78 gallons of champagne. Completely hand-wrought in silver and lined with gold, the only one of its kind in the world, it symbolizes a year's work for its creator, Julean Focan, world famous Belgium silversmith who also designs the Miss Universe, the Rose Bowl, and the Orange Bowl trophies.

This year's theme honors the 10th founding of the North Atlantic Treaty Organization (NATO). Encircling the bowl is the hand worked 15 flags and shields of the NATO nations, complete in every minute detail. Painstaking craftsmanship created the trophy; skill, excellence, and determination were the ingredients which won it. The trophy will become a permanent possession of the 54th, a lasting memento to the honor of the men who own it. Its monetary value, though very high, can never approach its symbolic worth for those men who gave of their toil during those hectic months when the squadron surpassed the efforts of every fighter organization throughout the USAF world.[66]

The public affairs office offered its own summary of the event:

Seven men, representing the Central Air Defense Force's 54th Fighter-Interceptor Squadron of Ellsworth AFB, South Dakota, stopped at Richards-Gebaur AFB to receive the congratulations of Col. George H.

Van Deusen, Deputy Base Commander, for being named the ADC's "Outstanding Fighter Squadron." The seven airmen were on their way to Miami, Florida, where they were presented the Hughes Trophy at the Night Fighters Association luncheon on 4 September. The award is presented annually to the outstanding fighter squadron in the ADC.[67]

A typed sheet from the Administration Section, 54th FIS, posted on the squadron bulletin board was titled "54th Fighter-Interceptor Squadron to be feted at Hughes Award Banquet":

> Over one thousand dignitaries and invited guests are expected to be on hand when the Hughes Aircraft Company of Los Angeles, California and the 54th Fighter-Interceptor Squadron of Ellsworth AFB join forces this Friday night at 6:30 p.m. in the 54th aircraft hangar to present the largest and most distinguished gathering of the fall season. The high point of the gala evening's festivities will be the official presentation of the $25,000 Hughes Achievement Award Trophy for 1959 to the new "World Champions of Air Defense," the 54th Fighter-Interceptor Squadron. To symbolize

Group photo of members of the 54th Fighter-Interceptor Squadron at Ellsworth AFB after winning the Hughes Trophy Award with an F-89J as backdrop and the Hughes Trophy as the centerpiece.
Courtesy Master Sgt. Robert O'Daniel

the occasion, top management officials from the Hughes Company will lead the squadron and their guests in a champagne toast from the newly won ten-gallon prize.

In preparation for the party, the 54th hangar (built to hold two Convair B-36 bombers, a very large aircraft with a wingspan of 230 feet and length of 162 feet), the only on-base facility large enough to harbor the expected throng, has been expertly decorated in such a manner that informed sources guarantee the huge structure will be barely recognizable in its original form. Earlier plans for a pair of giant, sky-sweeping searchlights placed outside the building had to be abandoned for fear of interference with incoming flights. Likewise, a suggestion for wet cement outside the front door for the footprints of those attending was discarded when it was pointed out that the 1,000 champagne imbibing guests were to leave an indelible mark without the benefit of soft concrete.

Inside, the evening's festivities will open with a martini-daiquiri, herring-shrimp cocktail hour followed by a succulent banquet: roast prime ribs of beef, baked Virginia ham, and young "Tom" turkey should provide the guests with a superb cuisine. Cocktail, dinner, and dancing music will be forthcoming from the "Melidoers" and the famed "Skyriders" orchestra.

Lt. Col. Ernest B. Nuckols, Jr., Commander of the 54th, has promised that the presentation ceremonies will be brief, and that the major emphasis for the evening will be placed on fun and gayety, animated by the enlivening spirits of bubbling, sparkling champagne. Expected among the guests are Major Dusek and a large number of city officials. Press and news media will be well presented by popular personages from KOTA, KRSD, the *Journal*, and *Black Hills Bomber*.

Brigadier General Loran D. Briggs, Commander 821st Air Division; Col. Francis W. Neye, Commander 28th Bomb Wing; and Col. Arthur George, Ellsworth AFB, Base Commander, along with other high-ranking dignitaries and guests will represent the base. Besides General Briggs, three other Air Force generals are expected to attend: Brigadier General Harold L. Neely, 29th Air Division Commander; Major General John D. Stevenson, new [at that time] Commander, Western Air Defense Force; and Brigadier General Wendell W. Bowman, new [at that time] Commander, Central Air Defense Force. Also on hand, of course, will be top management officials of the Hughes Company who have flown in especially for the occasion.[68]

September 1–5, 1959: Col. Nuckols and a representative group of the squadron attended the annual Air Force Association in Miami, where Gen. Lawrence S. Kuter presented to the squadron the Hughes Award.[69]

The history of the 54th FIS described personnel challenges faced around this time:

> Again, the most serious problem facing the Operations Section was the rapid turnover in experienced aircrew personnel. Date of Separation personnel and transfers with no replacement personnel contributed to this weakness. The radar observer problem was the most critical. On 30 June, the squadron had an assigned strength of 30 radar observers. By 5 July, this figure dropped to 27, by 3 August to 20 radar observers, and 19 radar observers by 31 August. By 5 September, there were only 16 radar observers available for duty, a new low, with no relief in sight, and 28 F-89Js to man in the event of an emergency. An urgent request for manning assistance to the 29th Air Division resulted in four experienced radar observers being assigned for 30 days temporary duty to the 54th FIS beginning on 16 September from the 15th FIS, Davis-Monthan AFB, Arizona. In addition, a radar observer from the 740th AC&W Squadron was permanently assigned to the 54th FIS. Five more radar observers were programmed for duty to the 54th FIS in September and October.
>
> Major flying training emphasis during the three months of 1 July to 30 September reporting period has been placed on radar runs against evasive action and ECM chaff dropped from the speed boards of target F-89Js, resulting in the first concentrated ECM aircrew training in over a year. In addition high altitude targets were pushed to 40,000 feet with a 15,000-foot snap up and both target and fighter speeds were increased substantially. These latter innovations were aimed at attempting a more realistic training program, even though it resulted in some loss in success rates. At this time, the Russian Air Force long-range Tupolev Tu-20 Bear has a service ceiling of 59,000 feet. The F-89J's maximum service ceiling of 49,000 feet with a snap up firing of conventional air-to-air missiles or nuclear fusion warhead Genie air-to-air missiles were within its altitude interception capabilities. F-89J flying time was distributed at 40 percent high level targets, 40 percent medium level targets, and 20 percent low level targets.
>
> Cross training of squadron aircrew personnel with the Air Division GCI sites had to be suspended for lack of radar observers. A shortage of GCI directors resulted in a reduction to one site per month visiting the 54th FIS squadron for training. During this period, "Cartoon" a new AC&W site, was included in this system and was provided live intercepts by the 54th FIS.
>
> Modification to the 54th FIS alert hangar for the follow on ADC alert aircraft, the Convair F-106 Delta Dart, necessitated a move by the Alert Force to the Ellsworth Operations Area on 14 September. A return to the alert hangar facility was programmed by the first week in December.

Squadron weapons handling efficiency was tested in two mass loads on 24 and 28 July. Results were determined to be satisfactory by the Squadron Commander, Lt. Col. Ernest B. Nuckols Jr.

The squadron engine shop established a world performance record by maintaining a J35-A-35 engine from an F-89J for 1104:30 hours without a major overhaul. A detailed check of available records at Headquarters, Oklahoma City Air Material Area, Tinker AFB, Oklahoma, revealed that no other J-35 engine has equaled this performance.

In a freak accident, First Lieutenant John R. Trulove received first and second degree burns when an inboard fuel cap exploded on engine run-up, spraying raw fuel into the rear cockpit which was ignited by engine exhaust. The incident occurred on 19 August. Lt. Trulove was transported by ambulance to the Ellsworth AFB hospital, stabilized, and then flown by air medical evacuation flight to the US Army Burn Center on 20 August at Fort Sam Houston, Texas. He received intensive treatment and was at the Burn Center for 90 days. The pilot, Lieutenant James B. Gormley, was uninjured.[70]

8–10 November: The squadron was given tactical evaluation by CADF.
3 December: A luncheon was held at the Sheraton Johnson Hotel for Gen. Lessig, enabling him to meet Rapid City businessmen.
7 December: Inspection team for USAF Headquarters was here. Headed by Gen. Stewart, they were primarily interested in our Special Weapons area.
16 December: Gen. Atkinson, Commander, ADC, arrived at Ellsworth to present the 54th FIS the USAF Safety Award.[71]

The history of the 54th FIS offers some further details of this period:

During the reporting period of 1 October to December 31, 1959, daily 54th FIS training in all phases of aircrew professionalism was maintained by the operations section through this three month period. The squadron Operations Officer was responsible for coordination of all aspects of squadron operations. During this reporting period Lt. Melvin Chubb took over instrument training phases and kept all pilots well qualified in the various aspects of instruments. The Operations Section also instituted weekly sessions of ground school lectures for all aircrews on Friday afternoons. In addition all flights maintained their own ground training.

The squadron remained well qualified in radar training with daily missions being flown to maintain a high degree of proficiency. During these sorties constant attention was devoted to tactics and close coordination between GCI and the aircrews. Results of the radar missions for the three months in terms of profiles and intercepts as recorded.

	Oct	Nov	Dec
Profiles attempted	208	194	178
Profiles successful	185	160	154
Intercepts attempted	590	687	629
Intercepts successful	543	596	561

The serious shortage in radar observers which had existed in the first part of this reporting period was alleviated by the arrival of new personnel. During the month of October it was necessary for four radar observers to be assigned to the squadron on a TDY basis because of the shortage. Monthly tactical exercise by the 29th AD enabled the squadron to train under situations of simulated combat. The daily training in radar missions paid off.

	Attempts	Made	Missed
8 October	18	16	2
13 & 14 October	31	30	1
4 November	2	2	0
9 November	16	13	3
23 November	2	2	0
3 December	7	5	2

Around the middle of October extensive modifications were begun on the alert hangar, and the squadron alert was pulled from the squadron's operations section. Because of the intense cold during the winter months in South Dakota, the alert status of the Genie aircraft was downgraded from 30 minute alert to one hour alert. Modifications on the alert hangar continued throughout this period, and a return to its anticipated location was delayed from December 1959 to January 1960. The old alert pads of two of the aircraft alert bays in the hangar were torn up and replaced. Inside extensive refurnishing was done, with the quarters being sound-proofed and revamped.[72]

The *Rapid City Journal* printed the following article describing some of the jargon used at this time by 54th FIS members:

Fanout! That's the 54th Fighter-Interceptor Squadron's way of shouting "extra." Or in the jargon of Ellsworth AFB's first line of defense from enemy attack, "ROLLERSKATE" has called "APPLEJACK." As the "Fanout" spread through the telephone lines in Rapid City and Ellsworth AFB last week, sleepy pilots, crewmen, and radar operators tumble out of bed. It was 3 a.m. and word had come to the 54th that enemy bombers were approaching Rapid City from the north. The same alert was flashed to fighter-interceptor units in an area ranging from

The 54th Fighter-Interceptor Squadron

Boise, Idaho, Filter Center for the 9th Air Division controlling airborne Air Defense Command fighters, including those of the 54th FIS. *United States Air Force Historical Research Agency*

Michigan through California. Rapid City's domestic scene was repeated at many cities and bases in the area.

Like many military operations, last week's exercise was a case of hurry up and wait. Crewmen of the 54th assembled at Ellsworth AFB within the hour and were ready to launch a full-scale assault on incoming planes. Ready planes are kept on constant alert at the squadron and could have been in the air within minutes. There is not frantic wheel spinning activity at the 54th as men await the word for take-off. Crews keep an eye on a schedule board in the ready room. Coffee cups, hanging on racks like old barbershop mugs, are in constant use. Some play cards, others take the opportunity to catnap. There are bull sessions everywhere. Countless exercises, similar to the one last week have honed the routine to the near apex of human perfection. Indications were that if the enemy had been real the level of excitement wouldn't have been much higher. Briefings are held to inform the pilots of weather conditions and the battle staff receives a steady flow of information from the ADC. Aircrews have checked their F-89J Scorpions and ground crews swarm over aircraft to check fuel and armament. When all is in readiness, there is just one thing to do, wait.

About two hours after the "fanout," the first Scorpion team takes to the air with instructions to "cap" over northern United States cities. These

F-89J on display at the National Museum of the United States Air Force. The white missile behind the right wing is a Genie that could be armed with a nuclear warhead to knock down penetrating enemy aircraft. *Author Photo*

pilots will circle the cities waiting for the "enemy" to approach. They may be relieved regularly by other planes or recalled if the exercise is cancelled or a full-scale alert is sounded and waves of Scorpions are sent into battle. Men of the 54th, like those in all ADC units throughout the nation, count their time in minutes. Each alert signal, whether it is "APPLEJACK" or "SNOWFLAKE," represents the minimum span of seconds necessary to "BRAKETIME" and take-off. Fuel supply is calculated to the minute and almost anybody in the squadron can tell time necessary to strap on a parachute and fire up a jet. While pilots and operators perform the most dramatic part of the exercise, their take-off is but the end product of endless education, drill and exercises by many men.

In the distant north and closer to home personnel of radar units scan the skies every hour of the day for aircraft and give accurate information on incoming planes. Intelligence teams, weather forecasters, maintenance crewmen, ground personnel and men in the tower all perform vital functions in a brief span of time before planes can leave the ground. Last week's exercise was a dual function. Not only was it part of continuing

The 54th Fighter-Interceptor Squadron

practice for the 54th, the alert also served to give B-52 crews a chance to determine defenses. F-89J Scorpions are two-place, twin-engine turbojets capable of carrying a literal arsenal of offense. The "J" series is capable to carrying nuclear-type, Genie air-to-air missiles. Next year, new two-place jets in the supersonic Century series are expected at Ellsworth AFB, according to unofficial sources. They will probably be the F-101B type airplanes. The 54th is the nation's leading fighter squadron and broke all existing records in recent exercises. Crews of the 54th returned from Arizona competition last year with 28 world records, not only taking first place among 47 other ADC fighter squadrons for air defenses. The feat of winning 28 world records has never been accomplished by any other ADC squadron.

    Evaluations were made on every phase of a mission, from assembly and loading to scramble procedures and firing at high-speed targets. Firing was in two parts: "dry" without weapons, and "wet" with weapons. The 54th ranks first nationally in both. Special accolades during the competition went to maintenance and radar crews. Maintenance men kept all 27 aircraft from Ellsworth AFB in the air both days of

the Arizona competition. And for two years the Arizona range had been in operation the 54th jets didn't have a single malfunction of radar equipment during evaluation passes. Radar and maintenance crewmen set 17 records of their own. The 54th FIS at Ellsworth AFB is the proud possession of the Hughes Trophy. Signifying their importance as fighting men.[73]

Flight Simulator Section stopped operation on May 3, 1960, for the purpose of dismantling the MB-39 Flight Simulator to the National Guard. The MB-42 Flight Simulator [for the F-102] was to replace the NB-39 that arrived on schedule from the contractor. This equipment was placed in storage due to the deactivation of the unit [no longer to replace the F-89J with the Convair F-102 Delta Dagger].[74]

Under the historical record of the 54th Fighter-Interceptor Squadron (ADC) for the period ending June 30, 1960, Ellsworth AFB, the following information indicated the status of the squadron:

F-106 on display at the National Museum of the United States Air Force. Prior to discontinuance, the 54th FIS was to trade in its F-98Js for F-106s. *Author Photo*

Equipment: (28) Northrop F-89Js and (2) Lockheed T-33As

a. During the three month reporting period, April 1, 1960 to June 30, 1960, the 54th Fighter-Interceptor Squadron participated in two tactical evaluations. One by the 29th Air Division and one by the ADC. An overall rating of "Outstanding" was received from the 29th Air Division and a "Satisfactory" rating received from ADC. This demonstrates the high level of professional achievement gained by the squadron and the desire to excel by all personnel assigned to the 54th FIS.

Through the continuation of daily training flights, the 54th Fighter-Interceptor Squadron has maintained its high level of aircrew and maintenance proficiency. During the last three months, the squadron has flown an increasing number of ECM and low-altitude intercept missions. On each training day, a chaff equipped T-33A was flown three to five miles in front of an F-89J target aircraft. Two flights of two aircraft each, executed snap-up attacks against this multi-target chaff environment. In addition, the squadron flew a greater number of sorties against SAC aircraft flying in the division area.

Original, hand-painted 54th FIS patch design for winning the 1959 Hughes Achievement Award. The drawing was donated to the South Dakota Air and Space Museum for display with its memorabilia of the 54th Fighter-Interceptor Squadron. *Courtesy Master Sgt. Robert O'Daniel*

b. Alert hangar modification.

Work has been started in the modification of the squadron's alert hangar for the F-106 aircraft. This involved increasing the size of the front and rear bay doors. [This was completed, but the new aircraft were never assigned to the 54th FIS.]

c. Flight simulator removed.

The MD-29 flight simulator was removed as part of the squadron's conversion to the F-106.

d. Awards.

The 54th Fighter-Interceptor squadron won the USAF Flying Safety Award for 8,000 accident free flying hours.[75]

Training was an important part of the 54th FIS, including deployments to forward operating bases. One such deployment was to Glasgow AFB, Montana, in June 1960. Such a deployment was more than just flying in aircraft from Ellsworth to Glasgow AFB:

Foreword

1. This plan is designated to establish uniform procedures for the movement and support of the 54th FIS from Ellsworth AFB, South Dakota, to Glasgow AFB, Montana, for a period of 45 to 60 days, starting on, or about, July 15, 1960.

Annex L, Services Facilities.

1. Welcome to Glasgow AFB. We hope you enjoy your stay with us even though we are still quite limited in respect to many of the facilities which you are used to enjoying at your home base.
2. This is a SAC base with the 13th FIS (ADC) 1904-1 AACS Det., Detachment 23-9th Weather Squadron, the 522nd FTD as tenants. Base duty hours are 0700-1100, 1200-1600. To assist you we have prepared the following items.
3. Glasgow AFB is located 20 miles north of the city of Glasgow. There is no rail or bus service so that all unofficial travel between base and the town has to be performed by private vehicle.
4. The city itself is small and has extremely limited recreational facilities, although there is a very pleasant recreational areas for fishing, swimming, boating and golf at Fort Peck, some 40-miles from the base.
5. Officers, while at Glasgow, will be expected to eat their main meals at the Officers' Open Mess instead of the airman's dining hall.
6. There is an Optimist Club on base which meets regularly every Monday at 1100 hours for lunch at the Non-Commissioned Officers' Mess and all Optimists are cordially invited to participate in our meetings.

1. General Situation.

A. The 54th Fighter-Interceptor Squadron, Ellsworth AFB, South Dakota, will be deployed to Glasgow AFB, Montana, on or about July 11, 1960 for a period of 45 to 60 days due to major runway construction at Ellsworth AFB.

B. The 54th FIS will deploy all available aircraft, including T-33 aircraft, for the duration of deployment: (28) F-89 and (2) T-33.

C. The 54th FIS will deploy 55 officers and 200 airmen; a total of approximately 255 personnel.

D. The 54th FIS will occupy the northeast nose dock for hanger, supply, and office space. Additional office space is available in the south-west nose dock on a permanent basis during the TDY period. The 54th FIS may use hangar space in the southwest nose dock unless this space is required to support a SAC aircraft.

E. 4141st Strategic Wing will furnish necessary support functions within their capabilities to include billeting, messing, medical, security, ramp space, hangar space, supply, transportation, POL, communications, and aircraft crash fire-fighting.

F. 13th FIS will furnish such field maintenance as within its capability.

2. Assumptions.

A. Runway construction will be completed within 60 days at Ellsworth AFB.

B. Upon completion of runway at Ellsworth, the 54th FIS will immediately return to that base.

C. Such personnel required to support the 54th FIS not available from the 4141st Strategic Wing. Resources will be augmented by 821st Air Division and/or 29th Air Division to include such support personnel as:

(1) Air police (5) each
(2) POl specialists (10) each
(3) Fire fighters (12) each
(4) Vehicle mechanics (6) each
(5) Supply technicians (3) each
(6) Field maintenance
   (a) Hydraulic specialist (1) each
   (b) Tire build up (2) each
   (c) Parachute packers (6) each
(7) Flight surgeon (1) each

D. 54th Fighter-Interceptor Squadron will be furnished a 60 day en route kit of all required supplies by the Base Supply Officer, Ellsworth AFB.

E. 54th FIS will bring all necessary aircraft support equipment to include towing units required for support of flying and maintenance.

F. Vehicles furnished on daily dispatch to 54th FIS by Ellsworth AFB will accompany unit. Drivers will be furnished by 54th FIS.

G. Additional POL vehicles (Search F-6 unit with tractors) will be furnished by Ellsworth AFB to Glasgow AFB.

H. Augmentation personnel and equipment will be merged under the control of the respective functional command for efficient utilization.

3. Tasks

A. 4141st Strategic Wing Staff will:

   (1) Deputy Commander Material.

     (a) Act as primary project officer.

     (b) Provide office space.

     (c) Provide parking space.

     (d) Coordinate with 13th FIS to provide field maintenance capability as available.

     (e) Provide re-servicing support.

     (f) Provide through 4141st Consolidated Group Supply, such office furniture as available.

   (2) Deputy Commander Operations

     (a) Provide a functioning base operations facility to include weather briefings and weather data as required.

   (3) Deputy Commander Services

     (a) Provide food service facilities.

     (b) Provide billeting of 55 officers and 200 airmen plus such augmentation support personnel. (billeted with functional organization).

     (c) Provide recreational facilities as available such as Service Club, Base Exchange, theater, NCO club, Officers Club, gym, recreational area at Fort Peck (swimming, fishing, boating and camp grounds).

     (d) Provide laundry exchange for billeting supplies.

4. Deputy Commander Law Enforcement

   (a) Provide security and law enforcement within existing capabilities, as augmented by 54th FIS.

   (b) Honor Ellsworth vehicle decals.

   (c) Honor Ellsworth personnel security badges.

   (d) House any 54th FIS personnel and prisoners (as required).

5. Director Commander Installations.

   (a) Provide crash and rescue services.

   (b) Provide routine maintenance.

6. Other staff agencies as appropriate.

   (a) Assume responsibility for ground safety.

   (b) Provide legal services.

   (c) Provide medical services with capabilities on a share-and-share-alike basis.

   (d) Provide casualty reporting as required.

   (e) Provide publications and blank forms as available.

   (f) Provide religious facilities and services as available.

7. 13th Fighter-Interceptor Squadron.

   (a) Provide field-maintenance capability as available.

   (b) Share alert facilities as required.

(c) Provide such ADC forms and publications as available.

(d) Make available "Hot Line" communications as necessary.

8. 54th Fighter-Interceptor Squadron will:

(a) Project officer will coordinate all requirements with 4141st Strategic Wing project officer.

(b) Provide an advance party to arrive Glasgow AFB one week prior to deployment consisting of two officers and 10 airmen.

(c) Provide off-loading personnel for aircraft, truck, or train to handle and segregate equipment and supplies.

(d) Furnish Glasgow location unit a postal locator card, DD Form 1175, for all personnel one week in advance of arrival of unit.

(e) Distribute personal mail to individuals, Glasgow AFB.

(f) Furnish Transportation Officer at Glasgow AFB all information on incoming shipments at earliest practical date to include air movement of personnel and equipment, rail and truck.

(g) Furnish Transportation Officer information for return transportation requirements at least two weeks prior to return to Ellsworth AFB.

9. 821st Air Division will coordinate with 29th AD to insure necessary augment personnel and equipment (not property of 54th FIS) are made available to support the mission.[76]

The 29th AD *Monitor* noted the 54th FIS move from Ellsworth AFB:

When the landlord hands you an eviction notice there is only one thing you can do. Pack up and go. This is exactly the situation the 54th Fighter-Interceptor Squadron was in when their landlord at Ellsworth AFB, South Dakota, the SAC, gave notice that they would have to leave at least 60 days while the runway was being repaired. The notice was not as emphatic as the usual eviction notice. They could stay if they wanted, but if the 54th was to continue to fly, they would have to go somewhere else.

When you are actively engaged in air defense, like the 1959 Hughes Trophy winning squadron is, you don't take a two months' vacation. You deploy to another base and resume your mission as fast as possible. The 54th FIS went to Glasgow AFB, Montana.

Lt. Col. Ernest B. Nuckols, Commander, 54th FIS: "We'll be back on our regular training schedule within three days. This is a lot to expect because when a fighter squadron goes TDY, there is a little more involved than just throwing a few things into a B-4 bag [A bag of heavy fabric with side pockets with zipper openings used as an aircrew flight bag for deployments.] With any other squadron three days is possibly the minimum time lapse, but with the 54th, it is the maximum."[77]

The 414th Squadron also took note of the 54th FIS' move:

What all is involved in a squadron deployment? The 54th FIS' authority on this question is Captain Joseph Petrol Jr., Deployment Project Officer.

Additionally, Major LeRoy Quacy, 54th FIS Maintenance Officer: "This is one of the smoothest deployments I have ever seen. And I have been involved in some 20 of them during my career."

Captain Petrl: "I had the task of planning the move of some 270 men and 150 tons of equipment. It was neither a simple task, nor was it just a one-man job. It required cooperation and teamwork and the 54th lacks neither of these. It also required considerable cooperation and support from their SAC landlord. The SAC support was excellent and they had their problems too, with their own flying units also deploying to other bases."

Captain Walter Rich, 54th FIS Intercept Officer: "The planning for a deployment of this type is much more difficult than planning a PCS deployment. I was involved in a deployment to Thule, Greenland, which was a PCS move. You take everything with you. In a move like this one you have to figure exactly what you need to take and how much."

The real test of the planning began on 15 July, when the first equipment was loaded onto rail cars. [At that time, Ellsworth AFB was served by an active rail line that could bring in special nuclear munitions, as well as load equipment for deployments throughout the United States. It was considered rapid movement for exercises or real world dispersal of aircraft against a Russian Air Force attack.] The loading headache belonged to Captain Dennis Winkels. His task was to determine what equipment would go by rail, by convoy, or by C-123 airlift. By Thursday, 13 July, one day before Colonel Nuckol's target date to resume training, all the F-89s were in place at Glasgow, some seven C-123s off-loaded cargo, and 270 troops were in place. With the exception of five rail cars which arrived that night, the 54th was back in business.

Colonel Nuckols: "When you have officers and airmen like I have, a commander doesn't have to worry. I knew the 54th would come through with flying colors."

Captain Pertl: "The move to Glasgow was pretty good, but we still have to return to Ellsworth. I sweated this move and I'll have to start sweating again before I've dried out from this one."[78]

The official record of the 54th FIS to ADC provides a detailed view of the last active training deployment of the squadron. Even though the squadron was scheduled to be disbanded, training continued up to the final deactivation date, with the concept that ADC squadrons would be equipped with the F-106 and maintained as active air defense units. After returning from its deployment to Glasgow AFB, Montana, the 54th FIS participated in Exercise Sky Shield BS—ADC's ORI of the 29th Air Division—again deploying aircraft to Minot AFB, North Dakota. These activities were conducted under the reality of pending

F-89Js of the 54th FIS on the flight line at Ellsworth AFB prior to deployment to Glasgow AFB, Montana. *Courtesy Master Sgt. Robert O'Daniel*

deactivation and the quarter closed with the first F-89J being ferried to Philadelphia Air National Guard's 111th FIS. There were a total of 677 flights, including 479 interception profiles, of which 363 were successful.

	July	August	September	Total
Profiles attempted	169	142	168	479
Profiles successful	130	110	123	363

After official ADC confirmation [orders] of squadron deactivation was received, 13 F-89Js were put through periodic maintenance before transfer. All F-89Js assigned to the 54th FIS were ready for transfer from Ellsworth AFB on October 14, 1960.[79]

The *Rapid City Journal* summarized the 54th FIS' time at Ellsworth AFB:

Rapid City and many residents of the Black Hills must bid a fond goodbye to the 54th Fighter-Interceptor Squadron. The men have changed and so have the planes but the 54th is a group which made some impact on the Black Hills. The story says the 54th FIS will be deactivated in October (1960). The story didn't say particularly that this represents progress but that is the picture as all those wise in the ways of defense know it. The men who flew the jets in the 54th were trained to get the plane up in the air and use radarscopes so that human error was minimized. The Nike units established near and around Rapid City will be demobilized also.

The emphasis must and should be on the mass of metal and machinery in the installation of the Titan I ICBM sites in the Black Hills. The projects are underway and progress is counted. The idea is that if such missiles are launched, then Red Moscow is a mess. This is a deterrent to war because the Russians know we would retaliate and not all the grim Kremlin group could escape. And an outlook for peace is only happy when we remember the facts.

The Russians never started a war because they didn't care.

The cost of peace has involved such units as the 54th for all the time it was stationed at Ellsworth AFB. It once was understood that some time might be needed to get some bombers aimed towards Moscow and it would be inconvenient if our bombers were clobbered on the ground. Simple facts forced the military as they worried about that simple matter and hence such planes as used by the 54th were developed. The 54th could aim a plane at an incoming target at a pretty fair speed and a rocket would find the target…rockets against rockets would be answer. But now the interim defensive weapons, including Nikes, are designed as garbage. The game of "war and peace" as Khrushchev and his masters and slaves play. It is vital because they think the United States might crumble. The propaganda that the Americans eventually will refuse to meet "Red" weapons with better weapons because taxes increase is heard from time-to-time.

It's possible there may be residents in the Black Hills who would say of the 54th…"I didn't like those guys 'or' who let that outfit go, I was getting about ten percent interest off a half-dozen?" There will be other words, the kind any one likes to have…"I'm sorry you're leaving, drop a card, come on back when you're out of the service, stop in anytime, keep in touch." Departure of the 54th is another phase of the transitions which Ellsworth AFB, and all of us, must accept.

The defense concept and the use and deployment of weapons has expanded through the years. It should be remembered that the runways are being expanded at Ellsworth AFB to accommodate heavy-laden aerial tankers. The tankers are required to serve the B-52s which fly around the clock and almost around the world so that they might converge in case a Communist dictator figured he'd smash the United States. We had bombers on the ground for quite some time when fighter pilots such as those in the 54th were required to protect "sitting ducks."

The program for each of the fighter pilots was important, and the importance of the 54th here and such units at every base surrounding the Soviet Union should never be underestimated. For the pilots, the officers in charge and for all the men who worked, we owe a tremendous vote of thanks. How many "scrambles" were made from the base here need not be counted, because it is impossible to count the thanks. The 54th was a good outfit. We can be proud of all the men and their families. We hope they will remember the Black Hills as friendly.[80]

The inactivation of the 54th FIS had significant coverage, including:

Another cutback in the number of personnel assigned to Ellsworth AFB is in the offing with the announcement on September 14, 1960, that the 54th Fighter-Interceptor Squadron with 460 men and 28 F-89J jet fighters will be deactivated in October. The 54th is one of two fighter-interceptor squadrons which will be deactivated as the result of revisions in the ADC program in the United States, the Air Force advised South Dakota Senator Francis Chase. The cutback will be offset, in part, by an increase in the number of Boeing KC-135A Stratotankers assigned to the 928th Air Refueling Squadron from 10 to 20. This will add approximately 200 men to that squadron for a net loss of Ellsworth personnel of 260. The increase in the number of tankers to be assigned at Ellsworth AFB had been previously announced. The Air Force informed Senator Case that personnel of the 54th will be reassigned to other Air Force activities. Senator Case asked the Air Force to consider the assignment of as many as possible to the Titan I ICBM squadron at Ellsworth to minimize moving disruption.

Inactivation of the 54th FIS follows a recent announcement that four Nike batteries of the Second Missile Battalion will be moved to other areas and replaced by one Nike-Hercules battery. Removal of the 54th FIS and the Nike-Ajax batteries is seen as a part of the changing concept of missile warfare. Accent is being placed on the deterrent effect and retaliation power of SAC's bomber and tanker squadrons and ICBM installations. An earlier move by the Air Force dispersed two of the B-52 squadrons of the 28th Bombardment Wing, which cut the number of personnel at Ellsworth by 1,200 to 1,300. The purpose of the dispersal program was to make more runways available to launch as many bombers and tankers as possible in event of an enemy attack.[81]

SSgt. Robert O'Daniel, an administrative clerk with the 54th Fighter-Interceptor Squadron—after the squadron was closed down—was transferred elsewhere with personnel and equipment. SSgt. O'Daniel moved 101 miles west to Sundance Air Force Station, Wyoming, remaining in the ADC business of protecting the United States. His description of Sundance AFS gives a look at how the F-89Js at Ellsworth AFB and other ADC bases were alerted to the possible presence of approaching Russian long-range bombers and guidance to within launch range of Genie AAMs:

The 54th Fighter-Interceptor Squadron heavily depended on electronic warning of possibly approaching enemy aircraft by radar squadrons throughout the area. An upgrade to the warning network was the 731st Radar Squadron at Sundance AFS Wyoming.

For all those assigned to the radar squadron, they received a welcoming pamphlet from the commander, at that time, Major Marvin C. Hamilton. As Commander of the 731st Radar Squadron, Sundance AFS:

Sundance Air Force Station on top of Warren Peak in the Bear Lodge Mountains north of Sundance, Wyoming. The three radar domes are easily recognizable. This is the operational area of the radar site. *Courtesy Master Sgt. Robert O'Daniel*

    I wish to extend to you a very hardy welcome. It is my desire, regardless of your duty assignment or length of stay with us to help make your assignment a very pleasant and gratifying tour of duty. Our squadron is the first of its type in the world; in that it is operationally powered by a nuclear reactor. I am proud to be the commander of this type installation and hope that you will assist us in maintaining the high standards established and constantly strive to better accomplish our mission.

    The mission of the 731st Radar Squadron, as part of SAGE, is to maintain and operate as part of the integrated ADC, within its area of responsibilities and to conduct the training required for the effective accomplishment of this mission.

    The radar site is located three and one-half miles northwest of the city of Sundance, Wyoming and 101 miles west of Ellsworth AFB, South Dakota.[82]

The first nuclear plant in the Air Force powered the Sundance Air Force Station.
Courtesy Master Sgt. Robert O'Daniel

Staff Sgt. (at that time) Robert O'Daniel, AFSC 70250, was assigned to the 731st Radar Squadron, Sundance AFS, Wyoming, from the 54th Fighter-Interceptor Squadron, Ellsworth AFB, South Dakota, on December 12, 1960. He actually departed Ellsworth AFB, PCS, on December 10 due to the advanced inactivation of the 54th FIS. Interestingly, when he arrived at the radar station, being an administrative specialist he sent reports on the operation of the nuclear power plant.[83]

The *Sundance Times* wrote the following about the nuclear power plant:

The nuclear power plant will also provide engineering and operating data for the design of improved power plants, which can be used at other Air Force installations. It was designed to provide factory assembled modules for air transport and quick assembly so nuclear power may be available any place in the world. The Atomic Energy Commission (AEC) will install and test-operate the plant for six months before transferring it to the ADC. The operating crew for the plant includes 17 airmen and an officer. All crew members are certified nuclear power plant operators.

As the 54th FIS was closed down, its air defense mission picked up by other ADC units, the radar station at Sundance AFS finished its one-of-a-kind upgrade to continue to support ADC defense of the Continental United States. The last four packages of 16-prefabricated units for the Air Force nuclear power plant at Sundance Radar Station arrived at Ellsworth AFB by air Friday, ready to be trucked to the Warren Peak site. The reactor is scheduled to achieve sustained chain reaction in September (1961). It will be cooled and moderated by "light" water and will be fueled with highly enriched uranium. When operational in 1962, it will provide 1,000 kilowatts of electrical power and 7,000,000 BTUs of heat per hour for the 731st Radar Squadron of the ADC's 29th Air Division, SAGE.[84]

A reactor specialist watches instruments at the Sundance Air Force Station. The atomic power plant was designed by the Atomic Energy Commission and built by military personnel. The operator is assigned to the US Navy. *Courtesy Robert O'Daniel*

The *Rapid City Journal* covered the construction and opening of Sundance:

A public ceremony was to be held in Sundance today [May 10, 1962] to formally open the Containment Area for the Sundance Radar Installation north of Sundance. The Containment Area, five-miles from Sundance, includes barracks, dining hall, bachelor officers' quarters, recreation building, power plant, and utilities buildings. The Operations Area is still under construction seven miles north of Sundance. During the ceremony the Containment Area was to be officially turned over to the Air Force. The program was to feature a flag-raising ceremony by the 731st Radar Squadron.[85]

The first nuclear power plant in the Air Force has gone into operation at Sundance AFS, climaxing months of construction and testing. In technical terms, the reactor "reached criticality," which means that control rods were withdrawn far enough so that a sustained chain reaction could begin. Representatives of the US Atomic Energy Commission said that tests would probably continue for several weeks before the reactor is brought up to full power. The nuclear power plant has been designated PM-1 for portable medium power plant. It was prefabricated by the Martin Corporation Nuclear Division in Baltimore, Maryland, under contract with the AEC and its component "packages" were flown west for reassembly at its mountaintop ADC site.

The first nuclear power plant to be used by the Air Force, PM-1 will produce about 1,000 kilowatts of electricity, enough for the normal needs of a community of 2,000. The electrical energy, however, is of unusually high quality, with voltage and frequency controlled within close limits under all conditions to protect the sensitive electronic equipment it will operate. The primary purpose of the reactor at Sundance is to provide electricity to power gigantic radar antennae. Search and detection of hostile aircraft is the primary objective of the Sundance AFS. It is an integral part of NORAD, the North American Air Defense Command. Besides electricity, PM-1 will provide an additional 2,000 kilowatts in the form of space heat for buildings occupied by the 731st Radar Squadron. The unit is part of the Minot SAGE (Semi-Automatic Ground Environment) chain which keeps a constant alert against possible enemy air attack.

The heart of the PM-1 system is a fuel core only three feet high and less than two feet in diameter. It consists of almost 750 stainless steel tubes, each half an inch in diameter, with about an ounce and a half of fissionable uranium enclosed with the walls of each tube. Water flowing through the core absorbs heat, and steam is generated through a heat exchange system to drive a turbine generator, producing electricity. The PM-1 plant is highly automated, so that it can be operated by as few as two people at one time. The assigned crew, however, includes 17 airmen and one officer to provide for around the clock operation. The group has been augmented by two qualified servicemen each from the Army and Navy.⁸⁶

The *Sundance Times* printed an article about the reactor at a later date:

The possibility of locating a temporary nuclear waste storage area in Fremont Country has stirred memories of Sundance residents who lived near a small nuclear reactor. In the height of the Cold War, the US Air Force built an experimental reactor to power three "radomes" that scanned the skies with radar searching for enemy missiles or aircraft. The project, known as the "Shield of Freedom," began operating in 1962 atop Warren Peak in the Black Hills National Forest, six miles from Sundance.

Harold Allen, Publisher of the *Sundance Times*: "The station pumped a lot of money into the area. And, we are still alive. Most of the people never worried about it. At the time, people were thrilled to have it here."

Many of those who worked at the radar site retired and remained living in Sundance. The employees and military personnel at the radar site were not issued dosimeters or badges that measured radiation. The radar site's secondary function was to serve as an operational experiment to see if a small nuclear reactor was a feasible power source for transport to a military installation in remote areas. But satellite technology rendered the site ineffective and costly, resulting in its closure and deactivation in 1968. It was part of the Cold War mentality with the concept of nuclear technology to provide better protection against a possible Russian nuclear attack. This was the only such installation installed by the Air Force, with cost becoming one of the primary reasons for not going ahead with additional installations and the reduction of ADC squadrons as the Cold War with the Soviet Union shifted from long range penetrating bombers to SLBMs and ICBMs.

More than two decades later, cattle and wildlife graze where only foundations are left as reminders of a nuclear-powered military complex. The land was returned to control of the US Forest Service.⁸⁷

The 29th AD posted the following statement:

The following ADC message, ADCMO-F-3 39484, to Headquarters USAF is quoted for your information:

Immediate action required by AFOCP-BU-PP, Subject: Discontinuance of the 54th FIS and the 58th FIS. Request DAF Letter AFMO 494-m, September 14, 1960 be amended to indicate December 18, 1960 as the discontinuance date for the 54th and 58th FIS. The extension is required to provide time to reassign personnel and close out supply accounts after the cessation of operations.⁸⁸

A 54th FIS F-86D in its alert bay at Ellsworth AFB facing the sunset toward the Black Hills. *Courtesy Master Sgt. Robert O'Daniel*

The Rapid City Chamber of Commerce's Military Affairs Committee sent the following letter to the 54th FIS:

> On behalf of the Rapid City Chamber of Commerce, the Military Affairs Committee wishes you are your men continued success in your future assignments. The 54th Fighter-Interceptor Squadron was a real credit to Ellsworth AFB, as well as the Rapid City area. We know your people have been an integral part of our community for a number of years. Those of your men that are to be reassigned will create a loss to numerous organizations within our community. We hope that future years will find opportunities for many of you to return to our area. Again, our best wishes to you and the men of the 54th Fighter-Interceptor Squadron.[89]

Headquarters ADC sent the following order to the commander, 54th Fighter-Interceptor Squadron at Ellsworth AFB, South Dakota:

> Discontinuance of Units," Colorado Springs, Colorado: United States Air Force, Ent AFB, General Order Number 140, September 22, 1960.
> I. Discontinuance of Units

Effective December 25, 1960, the 54th Fighter-Interceptor Squadron will be discontinued. Effective date of change of strength is December 25, 1960.

a. Personnel rendered surplus by this action will be reassigned according to separate instructions from this headquarters.
b. Equipment rendered surplus by this action will revert to stocks to fill present or future requirements.
c. Records will be disposed of in accordance with instructions contained in paragraph 040406, Air Force Manual 181-5.
d. Authority: Department of the Air Force Letter, AFMO 494m, September 14, 1960, Subject: Inactivation and Reorganization of Certain United States Air Force Units, as amended.[90]

EPILOGUE

The official record of the 54th FIS remains largely classified due to its nuclear mission. An editorial in *Rapid City Journal* summarized the mission of the 54th FIS, its importance to the defense of Ellsworth AFB, and its nuclear deterrence mission:

> Rapid City and many residents of the Black Hills must bid a fond goodbye to the 54th Fighter-Interceptor Squadron. The men have changed and so have the planes, but the 54th is a group which made some impact on the Black Hills.
>
> The story says the 54th FIS will be deactivated in [1960]. The story didn't say particularly that this represents progress, but that is the picture of all those wise in the ways of defense know it.
>
> The men who flew the jets in the 54th were trained to get the plane up in the air and use radar scopes so that human error was minimized.
>
> The Nike units established near and around Rapid City will be demobilized also.
>
> The program for each of the fighter pilots was important, and the importance of the 54th here and such units at every bomber base surrounding the Reds should never be underestimated.
>
> For the pilots, the officers in charge, and for all the men who worked, we owe a tremendous vote of thanks. How many "scrambles" were made from the base here need not be counted, because it is impossible to count thanks.
>
> The 54th was a good outfit. We can be proud of all the men and their families. We hope they will remember the Black Hills as being friendly.[1]

Remnant

A few F-89Js were saved from the scrap yard and moved to an aviation museum where the Cold War interceptor is on display. One 54th FIS F-89J (serial number 53-2453) is at the Heritage Flight Museum, Bellingham, Washington.

This F-89J was manufactured by Northrop Aircraft at its Palmdale, California, plant, and delivered to the Air Force on February 4, 1955. It was assigned to the 61st FIS (Northeast Air Command) at Ernest Harmon Air Base, Newfoundland. In August 1957, the aircraft flew to the Northrop plant for conversion to the "J" variant (able to deliver an air-to-air nuclear warhead). In December 1957, the 54th FIS received the modified aircraft. It served at Ellsworth AFB until the 54th FIS was deactivated. The aircraft was transferred to a series of bases: Vincent AFB, Arizona; Davis-Monthan AFB, Arizona; and Glasgow AFB, Montana. The aircraft serviced on with the Air Force National Guard, starting in October 1960, assigned to the 111th Consolidated Maintenance Squadron in Philadelphia. In April 1961, the aircraft was transferred to the 103rd FIS. In July 1962, the aircraft moved to the 186th FIS and 120th Fighter Group, both in Great Falls, Montana. The aircraft was dropped from active Air Force inventory, then transferred for possible acquisition by an aviation museum. The aircraft was used as a hands-on teaching airframe at the aviation maintenance school at Helena Regional Airport, Montana. It was later declared military surplus and offered for sale (auction). The Heritage Flight Museum won the auction, purchasing the aircraft for $600,122.[2]

After Ellsworth Air Force Base
Like the Phoenix rising from the ashes, the inactivated 54th FIS came out of deactivation and was redesignated the 54th Tactical Fighter Squadron (TFS) on January 13, 1987. The 54th TFS was reactivated on May 8, 1987, assigned to the 21st Tactical Fighter Wing (TFW) at Elmendorf AFB, Alaska. Redesignated the 54th Fighter Squadron (FS) on September 26, 1991, it was inactivated on April 28, 2000. During this time the 54th flew the McDonnell Douglas F-15C-30-MC Eagle.[1]

Elmendorf AFB was an important air-intercept base during the Cold War and continues this mission today as a resurgent Russian Air Force once again launches its long-range Tu-95M (60 remaining in operational status) Bear aircraft along the Aleutian Islands, probing US air defenses for responses. The author has termed this as the "New Cold War" between the United States and Russia. Elmendorf earned the nickname as "Top Cover for North America," protecting the air corridors from the Soviet Union into North America from attack by Russian Air Force long-range nuclear armed bombers. With the upgrade from the McDonnell Douglas F-4 Phantom to the F-15C, the 54th TFS, with its WWII history of fighting in the Aleutian Islands, was again stationed in Alaska in 1987. Early in 1990 the 21st TFW was replaced by the 3rd Wing. On April 29, 2000, the 54th FS was deactivated, with its F-15C/Ds transferred to the newly formed 12th FS.[3]

APPENDICES

APPENDIX A

Planes of the 54th FIS

Curtiss P-36A Hawk

Specifications and Performance Information

Wingspan	37 ft. 4 in.
Wing area	236 sq. ft.
Length	28 ft. 6 in.
Tail height	8 ft. 5 in.
Power plant	(one) 1,050 hp Pratt & Whitney R-1830 radial piston engine
Maximum speed	313 mph
Cruising speed	250 mph
Service ceiling	32,700 feet
Initial rate of climb	2,500 fpm
Range	830 miles
Empty weight	4,666 lb.
Combat weight	5,650 lb.
Armament	(two) .30-caliber machine guns or (two) .50-caliber machine guns
Crew	One pilot[1]

Nuke Msl

Curtiss P-36A Hawk on display at the National Museum of the United States Air Force, Wright Patterson AFB, Dayton, Ohio. *Author Photo*

The Curtiss P-36A Hawk was developed from the Curtiss Hawk Model 75, the direct forerunner of the famous Curtiss P-40 Warhawk. Production deliveries to the Air Corps began in 1938; eventually, the Army acquired 243 P-36As, including thirty undelivered P-36As intended for the Norwegian Air Force in 1942 under Lend-Lease. (After the German invasion and occupation of Norway these aircraft were diverted to US units.) The French Air Force used the Hawk 75A in combat against the Luftwaffe in 1939 and 1940, even though the fighter was obsolete compared to its primary opponent, the Messerschmitt Bf-109. In 1941, the Army Air Corps (AAC) transferred thirty P-36As to Hickam Army Air Force Base (AAFB), Hawaii, and twenty to Alaska. When the Japanese attacked US Navy and Army installations at and around Pearl Harbor, two of the first six Army Air Force (AAF) fighters to get off the ground were P-36s. With the outbreak of WWII, the US military's outmoded P-36s were relegated to training and courier duties within the United States. Many P-36s were sent to other countries under Lend-Lease.

Curtiss P-40E Warhawk
Specifications and Performance Information

Wingspan	37 ft. 4 in.
Wing area	236 sq. ft.
Length	31 ft. 9 in.
Tail height	12 ft. 4 in.
Power plant	(one) 1,150 hp Allison V-1710 inline piston engine
Maximum speed	362 mph
Cruising speed	235 mph
Initial rate of climb	2,190 fpm
Service ceiling	30,000 feet
Range	800 miles
Armament	(six) .50-caliber machine guns 700 lb. of bombs mounted underneath the wing
Auxiliary fuel	50 gal. centerline mounted drop tank
Crew	One pilot[2]

The Curtiss P-40 Warhawk was developed from the Curtiss P-36 and became the premier US fighter in service at the outbreak of WWII. P-40s engaged in aerial combat against Japanese Navy aircraft during the attack on Pearl Harbor and the invasion of the Philippine Islands in December 1941. They were flown in China by the Flying Tigers against the Japanese before the United States entered the war. P-40s were used in North Africa, including those flown by the first all-black fighter pilot unit, the 99th Fighter Squadron. P-40s served in numerous combat zones, including the Aleutians, Italy, the Far East, and the Southwest Pacific, and some were sent to Russia and used under Lend-Lease, even though often outclassed by its adversaries in the air in speed, maneuverability, and rate of climb.

Curtiss P-40 Warhawk on display at the National Museum of the United States Air Force, Wright Patterson AFB, Dayton, Ohio. *Author Photo*

Republic P-43 Lancer

Specifications and Performance Information

Wingspan	36 feet
Wing area	223 sq. ft.
Length	28 ft. 6 in.
Tail height	14 feet
Power plant	(one) 1,200 hp Pratt & Whitney R-1830-57 Twin Wasp radial piston engine
Maximum speed	356 mph
Cruising speed	280 mph
Service ceiling	36,000 feet
Range	650 miles
Empty weight	6,000 lb.
Combat weight	8,500 lb.
Armament	(four) .50-caliber machine guns (six) 20 lb. bombs, three per side, under wing
Crew	One pilot[3]

The Republic P-43 Lancer was delivered to the AAC in September 1940, but the Lancer was determined unsuitable for aerial combat, so they were converted into photo reconnaissance aircraft. The 150 converted/modified P-43Bs were supplied to the Royal Air Force under Lend-Lease.

Lockheed P-38 Lightning
Specifications and Performance Information

Wingspan	52 feet
Wing area	327 sq. ft.
Length	37 ft. 10 in.
Tail height	12 ft. 10 in.
Power plant	(two) 1,475 hp Allison V-1710 turbocharged inline piston engines
Maximum speed	414 mph
Cruising speed	275 mph
Service ceiling	40,000 feet
Range	1,100 miles
Empty weight	12,800 lb.
Combat weight	21,600 lb.
Armament	(four) .50-caliber machine guns (one) 22 mm cannon 3,190 lb. of ordnance on under wing pylons (two) 1,000 lb. bombs or (two) 1,600 lb. bombs or (10) 127 mm high-explosive unguided rockets
Crew	One pilot[4]

The Lockheed P-38 Lightning was designed in 1937 to perform as a high-altitude interceptor by 1939. In 1943, the fighter entered air combat against the Luftwaffe in North Africa. Equipped with dropable, auxiliary fuel tanks under the wings between the engine and fuselage, it became a long-range escort fighter.

Lockheed P-38 Lightning on display at the National Museum of the United States Air Force, Wright Patterson AFB, Dayton, Ohio. *Author Photo*

North American P-51 Mustang

Specifications and Performance Information

Wingspan	37 feet
Wing area	233 sq. ft.
Length	32 ft. 3 in.
Tail length	8 ft. 8 in.
Power plant	(one) 1,695 hp Packard-Merlin V-1650-7 inline piston engine
Maximum speed	437 mph
Service ceiling	41,900 feet
Range	2,000 miles
Empty weight	7,125 lb.
Combat weight	12,100 lb.
Armament	(six) .50-caliber machine guns (two) 1,000 lb. bombs or (six) 5-inch high-explosive unguided rockets
Crew	One pilot[5]

North American P-51D on display at the National Museum of the United States Air Force, Wright Patterson AFB, Dayton, Ohio. *Author Photo*

The 54th Fighter-Interceptor Squadron

Republic F-84E Thunderjet
Specifications and Performance Information

Wingspan	36 ft. 5 in.
Wing area	260 sq. ft.
Length	33 ft. 6 in.
Tail height	12 ft. 7 in.
Power plant	(one) 4,900 lb. thrust Allison J-35 turbojet engine
Maximum speed	620 mph
Initial rate of climb	6,000 fpm
Range	1,485 miles
Service ceiling	43,200 feet
Empty weight	10,180 lb.
Combat weight	15,220 lb.
Maximum Weight	22,400 lb.
Armament	(six) .50-caliber machine guns (eight) 5-inch high-explosive unguided rockets or 5,000 lb. of bombs or napalm tanks or 32 HVAR rockets
Crew	One pilot[6]

Republic Aircraft F-84 Thunderjet model on display at the South Dakota Air Space Museum marked in 54th FIS colors. *Author Photo*

Appendix A

North American F-86D Sabre Dog

Specifications and Performance Information

Type	Single-seat, all-weather interceptor
Manufacturer	North American Aircraft Company
Power plant	(one) 7,515-pound thrust, General Electric J47-GE-17B or J47-GE-33 turbojet engine with afterburner
Wing span	37 ft. 1 in.
Wing area	229 sq. ft.
Length	40 ft. 4 in.
Tail height	15 ft.
Maximum speed	706 mph
Range	835 miles
Service ceiling	54,600 feet
Empty weight	12,443 lb.
Combat weight	17,063 lb.
Electronics	AN/AGG-37 radar AN/APA-84 computer
Armament	(24) 70 mm "Mighty Mouse" Folding Fin Aircraft Rockets (FFAR) mounted underneath center-line fuselage
Crew	One pilot
Auxiliary fuel	(two) 120 gal. drop tanks, each with a strut base for stability, mounted under each side of the wing
Number built	25,04[7]

National Museum of the United States Air Force, "North American F-86D Sabre Dog," Dayton, Ohio, Wright-Patterson AFB. *Author Photo*

The 54th Fighter-Interceptor Squadron

Northrop F-89J Scorpion
Specifications and Performance Information

Type	All-weather, turbo-jet interceptor
Manufacturer	Northrop Aircraft, Inc.
Power plant	(two) 7,200 lb. thrust Allison J35 turbojets with afterburners
Wing span	59 ft. 8 in.
Wing area	650 sq. ft.
Length	53 ft. 10 in.
Tail height	17 ft. 7 in.
Range	1,364 miles
Maximum speed	634 mph
Initial rate of climb	8,350 fpm
Service ceiling	49,200 feet
Empty weight	25,142 lb.
Combat weight	42,152 lb.
Fire control system	E-6
Armament	
Conventional	(4) Hughes GAR-2 AAMs
Upgrade	(4) Hughes AIM-4 AAMs mounted in pods under the wing
Nuclear	(2) Douglas MB-1 Genie unguided, air-to-air missiles
Crew	Pilot / Radar observer[8]

Northrop F-89J Scorpion on display at the National Museum of the United States Air Force. *Author Photo*

Appendix A

F-89J (53-2550) assigned to the Des Moines Air National Guard, Des Moines International Airport, Iowa. On July 4, 1968, while I was a senior at Iowa State University, fourth year Air Force Reserve Officer Training Corps cadet, I attended an open house at the 134th Fighter Squadron, where one of the squadron's F-89Js was on display for the cadets. *Author Photo*

Had ride
Back seat

McDonnell Douglas F-15C Eagle
Specifications and Performance Information

Manufacturer	McDonnell Douglas Corporation
Current contractor	Boeing-Raytheon
Primary mission	Tactical/Air Superiority
Wingspan	42 ft. 10 in.
Length	63 ft. 10 in.
Height	18 ft. 6 in.
Power plant	(2) Pratt & Whitney 23,760 pound thrust F100-PW-220 afterburner turbofans
Maximum speed	1,650 mph (Mach 2.5)
Maximum range	3,450 miles
With	External conformal tanks and three external tanks
Service ceiling	60,000 ft.
Combat ceiling	65,000 ft.
Zoom-to-climb	98,400 ft.
Climb rate	50,000 fpm.
Empty weight	28,160 lb.
Maximum take-off	68,000 lb.
Electronics	Nose-mounted Hughes APG-70 radar for long-range shoot down of hostile targets
	Multi-function cockpit displays
	Tracor AN/ALE-45 chaff and flare dispenser
	Central digital computer
	Programmable Armament Control Set
	Tactical Electronic Warfare System
	ALR-56 radar warning
	ALQ-138 countermeasures
	Identification friend or foe
Upgrades	BLOS Satcom
	Targeting pod
	Eagle Passive/Active Warning System (EPAWSS)
Armament Combinations	(1) 20 mm M61A1 Vulcan cannon
	Up to four AIM-9 Sidewinder AAM
	-or- Up to four AIM-120 AMTRAAM
	-or- Up to 1,500 lb. of bombs, air-to-ground rockets, and air-to-ground and/or AAMs.
Life cycle	Through 2030
Crew	One pilot[9]

Appendix A

McDonnell Douglas F-15C Eagle on static display at Ellsworth AFB during the open house and air show Dakota Thunder 2000. *Author Photo*

The McDonnell Douglas F-15 Eagle is an all-weather, extremely maneuverable tactical fighter designed to permit the Air Force to gain and maintain air supremacy over the battlefield as an air superiority intercept fighter. In an air intercept role the F-15 is ideally suited for the long-range air superiority mission in Alaska.

APPENDIX B

54th FIS Integrated Air Defense of Ellsworth Air Force Base

54th FIS F-89Js could be armed with the McDonnell-Douglas AIR-2A Genie air-to-air missile. For training missions, the F-89J carried the ATR-2, a full-size Genie with an inert rocket motor and a live nuclear fission warhead replaced by an inert, training warhead. Its weight was the same as the nuclear variant.

The 54th FIS' previous interceptor was the F-86D, armed with unguided rockets that were to be fired into massed Russian Air Force bomber formations penetrating through Canada into the northern United States. Initial efforts to electronically guide the Genie to an airborne target had not been perfected by the late 1950s, so the Air Force opted for an unguided nuclear fission warhead air-to-air missile with a sufficient blast radius to knock down Russian bombers as far as possible from SAC bases, hopefully at a distance of 650 miles (one half the range of the F-89J, although in a real shooting war this more than likely would be extended to fuel exhaustion).

Hughes AIM-4 Falcon Air-to-Air Missile (AMM)

Specifications and Performance Information

Manufacturer	Hughes Aircraft
Designation	Air to air missile
Length	78 in.
Wingspan (fins)	20 in.
Diameter	6.4 in.
Weight	119 lb.
Speed	Mach 3.0
Range	Six miles
Guidance	Semi-active radar homing
	Rear-aspect infrared homing
Warhead	7.6 lb. (high explosive)[1]

Appendix B

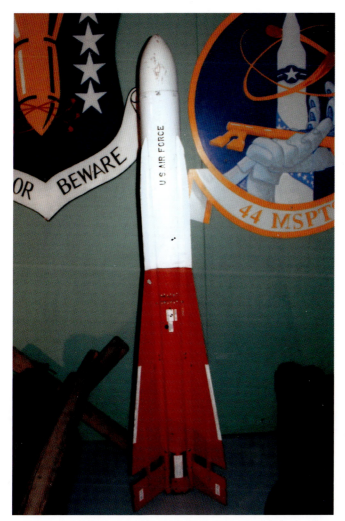

Hughes Falcon air-to-air missile on display at the South Dakota Air and Space Museum. *Author Photo*

The Hughes AMM-4 Falcon was the Air Force's first operational AAM. Development began in 1946, it was test fired in 1949, and was operational with ADC in 1956. It was initially designated GAR-1 and GAR-2 (1956). The 54th FIS' standard armament was four of these AAMs—two under each wing. The GAR-1 was equipped with a semi-active radar homing warhead with a short range of five miles, considered a close in weapon. GAR-2 (redesignated AIM-4B) was fitted with a heat seeking warhead for attacks from the rear against Russian Air Force bombers and turbojet fighters. The F-89J crew fired its two GAR-2s in salvo, followed by a salvo of two GAR-1s. The salvos were considered necessary because the weapon only had a sixteen pound conventional warhead without a proximity fuse, with a direct hit necessary to detonate the warhead.

McDonnell-Douglas AIR-2A Genie
Specifications and Performance Information

Manufacturer	Douglas Aircraft Company
Wingspan (fins)	3 ft. 4 in.
Length	9 ft. 8 in.
Diameter	17½ in.
Weight	822 lb.
Power plant	Thiokol SR-49 rocket engine
Propellant	Solid fuel
Thrust	36,500 lb.
Maximum range	Six miles
Maximum speed	Mach 3.3
Deployment	1957–1985
Number produced	3,150
Fire control	Targeting, arming, and firing coordinated by the launch aircraft's fire control system
Warhead detonation	Time delay fuse
Safety	Fusing mechanism would not arm the nuclear warhead until engine burnout
Blast radius	1,000 feet
Warhead	W-25 nuclear fission
Yield	1.5 kt.
Length	26.6 in.
Diameter	17.4 in.
Weight	218 to 221 lb.
Composition	Uranium and plutonium sealed pit
F-89J armament	
Nuclear	(2) AIR-2As
Conventional	(4) Hughes GAR-2 AAMs
Upgraded	(4) Hughes AIM-4 AAMs[2]

Rare inert Genie air-to-air missile on its transport dolly. Used for training of munitions, security, maintenance, and flight line personnel. Its electronics mirrored a real missile in flight operation. On display at the South Dakota Air Space Museum. *Author Photo*

54th FIS F-89Js, if loaded with Genies and launched in response to a Russian Air Force bomber attack, had the mission to intercept the bombers and knock them down prior to being able to drop their nuclear bombs. If the nuclear fission warheads on the Genie missiles did not knock down the bombers, the aircrew would track individual bombers, locking on with their radar and launching conventionally armed air-to-air missiles. Each F-89J carried four of these missiles.

If Russian bombers somehow escaped the intercepting F-89Js, the 54th FIS aircraft were backed up by four Army Nike-Ajax surface-to-air missiles protecting Ellsworth AFB. In conjunction with the 54th FIS, the Army's Nike-Ajax Headquarters and Headquarters Battery, 2nd Missile Battalion, 67th Artillery had four missile launch sites around Ellsworth AFB. Along with the 54th FIS, the Nike-Ajax batteries formed the Ellsworth AFB Defense Area (EDA). Radar guidance for the 54th FIS and the Nike-Ajax missiles was overlapping and provided for the interception of Russian bombers.[3]

The 54th Fighter-Interceptor Squadron

~~Nike-Ajax~~ Surface-to-Air Missile

Specifications and Performance Information

Prime contractor	Western Electric
Airframe contractor	Douglas Aircraft (Missile Division)
Power plant contractor	Aerojet Corporation
Booster contractor	Bell Aircraft
Designation	MIM-3
Overall length	34 ft.
Without booster	21 ft.
Wing span (fins)	4 ft.
Diameter	12 in.
Launch weight	2,458 lb.
Without booster	1,150 lb.
Maximum speed	Mach 2.2
Speed at burn out	1,669 mph
Maximum slant range	20 to 30 miles (note, considered close-in, point defense of last resort)
Maximum ceiling	60,000 ft.
Upgrade	72,000 ft.
Booster	Solid propellant
Thrust	50,000 lb.
Duration	2.8 seconds
Sustainer	Liquid fuel

Tested & proven

US Army Nike-Ajax surface-to-air missile on its erector/launcher. Training missile transferred from one of the four former active missile batteries circling Ellsworth AFB for point or close in air defense. On display at the South Dakota Air Space Museum. *Author Photo*

Thrust	2,600 lb.
Duration	21 seconds
Warhead	High explosive (conventional)
Combinations	12 lb.
	122 lb.
	179 lb.[4]

The Nike-Ajax's conventional warheads were designed to take out one airborne target per missile and were stored in Ellsworth AFB's WSA—rotated through the four Nike-Ajax sites, each with sixteen missiles. Each site had four alert missiles with twelve reloads. The 54th FIS' F-89Js were the first line of defense, with the Nike-Ajax missiles the final point of defense of Ellsworth AFB. This was a Cold War mentality that nuclear weapons were just larger yield detonations for the Genie than high explosive Nike-Ajax warheads. Interestingly, there was no consideration or tactical discussions about what if the Russian bombers dropped to low level, separated, and approached designated targets instead of mass bomber formations at high altitude.

The Air Force could not arm the Nike-Ajax with a nuclear fission warhead. After the Cuban Missile Crisis, around Ellsworth AFB the four Nike-Ajax missile sites were deactivated and replaced by one Nike-Hercules surface-to-air missile site. The Nike-Hercules supported the 54th FIS up to the squadron's deactivation in October 1960.

Nike-Hercules Surface-to-Air Missile

Specifications and Performance Information

Prime contractor	Douglas Aircraft (California)
Booster contractor	Hercules Powder Company (Radford Arsenal, Virginia)
Sustainer motor Contractor	Thiokol Chemical Corporation
Guidance contractor	Western Electric
Designation	MIM-4
Overall length	41 ft. 6 in.
Without booster	27 ft.
Wing span	6 ft. 2 in.
Diameter	2 ft. 6 in.
Firing weight	10,560 lb.
Without booster	5,250 lb.
Booster	Cluster of four solid propellant boosters
Propellant	Solid fuel
Sustainer	Solid propellant
Maximum speed	Mach 3.5
Speed at burnout	2,597 mph
Maximum slant range	75 to 90 miles
Maximum ceiling	100,000 feet

Warhead combinations

Conventional	High explosive
Nuclear	W-7 (initial)
Yield	2 to 40 kilotons
Upgraded	W-31
Yield	Low (2 kilotons)
	Medium (20 kilotons)
	High (30 to 40 kilotons)[5]

Appendix B

US Army Nike-Hercules surface-to-air missile. At Ellsworth AFB, one battery of Nike-Hercules replaced four Nike-Ajax batteries. *US Army Aviation and Missile Command, Photo Archives, Historian Office*

APPENDIX C

54th FIS Commanders

Commander	Date of Command
1st Lt. K. A. Tyler	1-15-1941 to 1-29-1941
2nd Lt. C. J. Looke	1-19-1941 to 2-9-1941
2nd Lt. T. W. Jackson	2-9-1941 to 2-18-1941
1st Lt. W. Lane, Jr.	2-18-1941 to 3-4-1941
1st Lt. H. D. Aynesworth	3-4-1941 to 3-12-1941
1st Lt. W. Lane, Jr.	3-12-1941 to 3-15-1941
Capt. K.S. Wade	3-15-1941 to 3-18-1941
1st Lt. H.D. Aynesworth	3-18-1941 to 3-24-1941
1st Lt. W. Lane, Jr.	3-24-1941 to 4-18-1941
2nd Lt. B. Irwin	4-18-1941 to 5-1-1941
Maj. T. W. Jackson (KIA)	5-1-1941 to 9-14-1942
1st Lt. Victor E. Walton	9-14-1942 to 9-20-1942
Maj. Ashkin	9-20-1942 to 10-27-1942
Capt. Francis Pope	10-27-1942 to 1-9-1943
Capt. Morgan H. Griffin	1-9-1943 to 7-18-1943
Capt. William Samways	7-18-1943 to 7-25-1945
Maj. Ardis	7-25-1945 to 10-9-1945
Maj. Harrison	10-9-1945 to 12-1-1945
1st Lt. Preble	12-1-1945 to 1-1-1946
1st Lt. Bickett	1-1-1946 to 3-1-1946

Note: 54th FIS inactive until December 1, 1952

Commander	Date of Command
Lt. Col. Paul J. Imig	12-1-1952 to 9-18-1953
Lt. Col. W. F. Benedict	9-18-1953 to 3-25-1954
Maj. William H. Fairbrother	3-25-1954 to 2-15-1956
Lt. Col. Herbert O. Schulze	2-15-1956 to 1-1-1957
Maj. Alma R. Flake	1-1-1957 to 5-15-1959
Maj. James C. Brown	5-15-1959 to 7-14-1959
Lt. Col. Ernest B. Nuckols Jr.	7-14-1959 to 12-25-1960[1]

APPENDIX D

54th FIS Participation in Operation Plumbbob "Shot John" July 19, 1957

Two F-89J pilots and two radar operators (ROs) were tasked to participate in the testing of an atomic warhead on a Genie AAM. They flew two 54th FIS T-33s to Kirkland AFB to become part of the 4950th Test Group (nuclear), temporarily assigned to the Air Force Special Weapons Center, 4926th Test Squadron (sampling). Four F-89Js (only one conducted the live fire detonation) from operational ADC squadrons were selected for the test, with the two 54th FIS crews as backup. The 54th FIS aircraft were tasked to conduct effects studies. They would be airborne during the test detonation to determine the effectiveness of the weapon against possible Russian bombers. They were to fly through the resulting radiation cloud to measure levels of possible contamination.

During 1957, a series of 29 above-ground US nuclear tests were conducted at the Nevada Test Site (NTS), only 65 miles northwest of Las Vegas, Nevada. At that time, scientific calculations determined there would be no fallout radiation to the population of Las Vegas and the surrounding areas. The Las Vegas population

Northrop F-89J Scorpion model on display at the South Dakota Air Space Museum marked in 54th FIS colors. *Author Photo*

was not warned of the time nor the size of each nuclear test detonation. The Air Force was particularly interested in the effects of an airborne nuclear detonation on its ADC aircrews. The Air Force wanted to collect data on what would happen when an F-89J fired a live nuclear tipped warhead Genie AAM against a simulated area containing Russian Air Force long range bombers.

The "John Shot" on July 19, 1957, was the only test firing of the Air Force's AIR-2 Genie with a nuclear warhead from an air interceptor type aircraft in NTS Area 10. The Genie carried a 1.5 kiloton W-25 nuclear warhead powered by a Thiokol SR49-TC-1 solid fuel rocket engine with a thrust of 36,500 pounds. The W-25 was a Los Alamos Scientific Laboratory designed anti-aircraft warhead. It was produced 1957–1962, with 3,150 produced. It had a range of slightly under 6.2 miles. Targeting, arming, and firing of the weapon were coordinated by the launch aircraft's fire control system. Detonation was by time delay fuse, although the fusing mechanism would not arm the warhead until after engine burnout, giving the launch aircraft sufficient time to turn and escape. Lethal radius of the blast was approximately 1,000 ft.

The nuclear armed Genie was fired by Air Force Capts. Eric William Hutchison (pilot) and Alfred C. Barbee (RO) over Yucca Flats at 18,500–20,000 ft. above mean sea level. The launch was executed from aircraft serial number 53-2547. The rocket quickly accelerated to Mach 3.0, traveling 2.6 miles from the launch aircraft in 4.5 seconds, at which time the W-25 warhead was detonated by an

F-89J (53-2547): another aircraft took the photograph the moment the Genie was launched over the Nevada Test Site. As soon as the missile cleared the aircraft the F-89J executed a turn to the right, diving to reach a safe distance. *United States Air Force*

electronically coded (secure) signal from the ground control blockhouse. This distance was closer than supposedly planned for the interception of Russian bombers at a range of approximately six miles. The aircrew would turn away from the oncoming Russian bombers and attempt to reach safe distance before the airborne atomic detonation, escaping the airborne shock wave, gamma and neutron radiation, and the electromagnetic pulse wave that could burn out onboard electronics and communications equipment. The detonation was recorded as a yield of 1.7 kilotons.

One of the Air Force installations wanting information from this test was the engineers at Warner Robins Air Logistics Center (now Robins AFB, Georgia, Air Force Material Command. They still are responsible for weapons maintenance and repair.) During these nuclear tests the logistics center was responsible for all F-89 communications and fire control systems. The primary concern was what would be the effects on the aircraft's electronics from the EMP, neutron, gamma ray and other radiation bursts. A secondary concern was the shock wave impact on the aircraft as it turned away from the point of detonation. The 54th FIS had two aircrews and ground support personnel at these test detonations to provide information on their war fighting mission. They only had one collection effort, since this was the first and only firing of a live nuclear armed anti-aircraft missile.

A group of five Air Force officers volunteered to stand hatless, wearing light tan summer uniforms underneath the airborne blast to prove the weapon was safe for use over populated areas. Gamma and neutron doses received by observers on the ground were negligible. Radiation doses received by aircrews were highest for those in the airborne sampling aircraft assigned to penetrate the airborne detonation cloud ten minutes after detonation.

Upon landing, the aircraft—including the 54th FIS T-33s—were parked in a decontamination area. Environmental suited ground personnel sprayed the aircraft with soap, hosed off the soap, and then with another rinse cleaned the aircraft one more time. Once the aircraft were parked in a segregated aircraft parking apron, dosimeters were used to check the aircraft, then the aircrew were allowed to deplane. They were also checked with dosimeters, handing their radiation badges to technicians who recorded the number of REMs (radiation dose).[1]

APPENDIX E

In Memorium

The motto "Freedom is not free" applied to all members of the 54th FIS and support aircrew who suffered the ultimate cost while defending their country.

The citizens of Rapid City created a memorial to those who died while assigned to Ellsworth AFB (and its previous base names), including those assigned to the 54th FIS.

Line of 54th FIS F-89Js on the flight line at Ellsworth AFB. *Courtesy Master Sgt. Robert O'Daniel*

Appendix E

Granite stone marker given by the citizens of Rapid City to memorialize those who died at Ellsworth AFB. *Author Photo*

Memorial plaque for the F-51 crash. *Author Photo*

From *Rapid City Journal*:

Air Force officers are investigating yesterday's [February 15, 1951] crash of a F-51 fighter plane which claimed the life of First Lieutenant Kenneth Frank. [His crash and death is included with the 54th FIS because the 175th FIS was assigned to Ellsworth AFB for stop gap interceptor coverage until turbojet fighters and another unit could be assigned to protect the SAC base.]

Airmen were working today [February 16, 1951] to recover the body from the plane which slammed into the ground at the Corllss Jensen ranch four miles east of Farmingdale at 1:18 p.m. The plane set fire to pastureland and a strip of grass about 100 yards wide and a mile long burned before neighbors and air base personnel extinguished the blaze. [Grass fires could spread rapidly during the summer fire season in the Black hills and volunteer fire departments were always on call to respond to these fires before they could get out of hand. This fire was fought by the local fire department and fire engines responding from Ellsworth AFB. The base fire department was trained to fight aircraft fires and handle the potential dangers on military aircraft.]

Authorities at the base [Ellsworth AFB Public Affairs] said positive identification of the dead pilot has not been made, but "it is presumed to be Lt. Frank."

The pilot was a member of the 175th Fighter Interceptor Squadron [forerunner of the 54th FIS assigned to Ellsworth AFB], formerly a South Dakota Air Guard unit which was called to active duty and transferred from Sioux Falls to Rapid City last spring. World War II US Marine Corps fighter ace Joe Foss organized the unit which is now under the command of Colonel Duke Corning. Lieutenant Frank was one of the original members of the outfit and moved his family to Rapid City when the 175th was assigned to the local base.[1]

Also from *Rapid City Journal*:

A 23 year-old pilot from Astoria, Oregon, became the first casualty for the 54th Fighter Interceptor Squadron here [Rapid City]. His F-84 smashed into the ground two miles southeast of Ellsworth AFB last night [June 10, 1953].

It is believed he was instantly killed when Second Lieutenant Elmer M. Koski's Thunderjet crashed and exploded at 11:15 p.m. He was on a routine night training mission when the mishap occurred. First reports indicated he was coming in for a landing.

Residents in the vicinity said the explosion lit up the sky and others were awakened by the noise.

Lieutenant Koski was assigned to the 54th FIS here in September 1952. The 54th succeeded the 175th South Dakota Air Guard as a defense

Appendix E

Memorial plaque for the F-84 crash on June 10, 1953. *Author Photo*

Memorial plaque for the F-84 crash on June 23, 1953. *Author Photo*

squadron at the base and began the conversion from the 175th's F-51 propeller driven aircraft to jets last fall.

Lieutenant Koski joined the Air Force in January 1951, and after cadet training was assigned to Reese AFB from May 10 to September 17, 1952. He was converted to a jet pilot here in December last year.[2]

Capt. Wallace Cobb's death was in *Rapid City Journal* as well:

The second crash of a jet from the 54th Fighter Interceptor Squadron at Ellsworth AFB here within two weeks brought death yesterday [June 22, 1953] to Captain Wallace L. Cobb.

The 30-year-old pilot was probably killed instantly as ranchers in the area described an explosion in the air about 1:30 p.m., shortly after Captain Cobb had made his last radio report to Ellsworth AFB.

The scene was approximately 15 miles west of Faith, South Dakota, and a mile north of Highway 212 in rugged prairie country. The first man to reach the wreckage said the F-84 apparently plunged into a side hill and disintegrated. Debris was strewn around for more than 1,000 feet.

Captain Cobb was a veteran of World War II and was recalled to active duty on June 26, 1951. [The military call up of US military reserves during the Korean War, 1950–1953). He had been assigned to the 54th FIS only a short time.

The first Thunderjet fatality occurred on June 10, 1953, on the eve of President Dwight Eisenhower's arrival in the Black Hills. [On June 13, 1953, President Eisenhower landed at Ellsworth AFB to conduct a ceremony changing the base's name from Rapid City AFB to Ellsworth AFB. The name change honored the death of Brig. Gen. Richard E. Ellsworth, who lost his life in Newfoundland during the crash of a Convair RB-36H crash (aircraft number 51-13721) on March 18, 1953, along with the entire crew onboard.] Second Lieutenant Elmer M. Koski hurled into the ground two miles from the base and was instantly killed.

The latest mishap brought a widespread air and ground search when Captain Cobb failed to check in after reporting his position near Maurine yesterday afternoon [June 22, 1953].

About 3 p.m., Civil Air Patrol planes started circling over the approximate area but were forced to return to Rapid City at dusk when no trace of the plane was sighted. The search was resumed this morning [June 23, 1953] by air and ground and the wreckage was spotted at approximately 7:30 a.m.

Ranchers from Faith and Maurine vicinity, Nell Crowley, Faith Police Chief, and a ground part of an Air Force search and rescue team from Lowry AFB, Denver, combed the rugged country. Lyn Farnham rode to the wreckage from his ranch this morning as Gerry Snedlgar flew his plane over the site at the same time. Crowley said he had driven within a few miles of the spot yesterday afternoon without sighting the crash.

The air search was hampered this morning by heavy overcast. Snedlgar said he was flying about 100 feet above the ground when the remains of the F-84 were seen on the side of a hill.

CAP planes circled over the area to direct the rescue team to the site and also radioed the find to the Lowry rescue plane, which was about 20

Appendix E

minutes coming to the crash site. Meanwhile, Snedlgar and Randy Hill landed nearby and walked to the hillside, verifying the pilot was dead.

Captain Cobb's experience as a pilot dated from World War II. He had attended training school in Arizona before returning to Ellsworth AFB. This mishap occurred on a routine training mission. Captain Cobb had taken off with another Thunderjet but that pilot aborted and returned to base.[3]

The loss of Capt. Baker and A3C Countess as reported by *Rapid City Journal*:

Death claimed two men from Ellsworth AFB in separate accidents in the barren prairie country 60 miles northeast of Rapid City yesterday [February 15, 1955].

Captain David E. Baker, 33, was killed about 3:15 p.m., when he rode his Saber jet too close to the ground before bailing out.

The second victim was Airmen Third Class [A3C] Stanislaus Countess, age 17, thrown from a helicopter when it crashed at 9 p.m. en route to the scene of the jet disaster. Engine trouble was blamed for both mishaps.

Captain Baker had radioed he was having engine trouble while on a routine training mission and indicated he would try to bring the F-86D

Memorial plaque for the F-86D and H-9 crash. *Author's Photo*

back to base. His last message was that he was abandoning the plane. The ejection seat hurled him from the fighter but apparently he had waited too long and his parachute failed to open and save him. Captain Baker's body was found about three miles from the wreckage of his plane.

A3C Countess was one of five men aboard the helicopter. The others suffered minor cuts and bruises. The helicopter was being used to speed liaison between the base and the jet crash site. The injured included Lieutenant Colonel John Stephens, operations officer; Major John Malley, a B-36 aircraft commander from the 717th Bomb Squadron, 28th Bomb Wing; First Lieutenant Dean Martin, helicopter pilot and Airman First Class Ernest O'Brien of the air police. A3C Countess also was assigned to the 28th Police Squadron.

Captain Baker, a flight leader of the 54th Fighter Interceptor Squadron at Ellsworth AFB, was a Korean War veteran. He had flown 20 combat missions there in F-51s. He was assigned to the 54th FIS about two years ago.

A3C Countess had been at the base only a short time.

Blizzard weather in the open country where the F-86D and the H-19 helicopter crashed hampered recovery efforts during the flight and today.

A truck and ambulance convoy started to the area during the night. The four helicopter survivors spent the night at Mud Butte and suffered no ill effects before returning to the base, where they will get a routine medical check late this afternoon.

The two crashes were 20 miles apart. The helicopter hit the ground three miles east of Mud Butte, while the jet crashed two miles south of Stoneville. It was the second flight for the helicopter and apparently the pilot had difficulty locating the jet.

Before the storm moved in to virtually halt all travel to the area, Major William Fairbrother, commanding officer of the 54th FIS, had warned civilians to stay away from the scene, as the jet was loaded with rockets.

Gusty winds and snow moved into the area shortly before this helicopter accident.

Captain Baker's death was the third fatality for the 54th FIS.[4]

APPENDIX F

The 54th FIS Carries on at the South Dakota Air and Space Museum

The 54th FIS maintained its ADC alert mission 1951—1960. The historical significance of the ADC mission is preserved with the first generation Butler aircraft alert hangar and alert supporting structures. The alert hangar was moved off-line for the South Dakota Air and Space Museum. When the 54th FIS was inactivated at Ellsworth AFB, the primary four-bay alert facility was removed and several support buildings were heavily altered for other base purposes. The 28th Bomb Wing renovated the Readiness Crew dormitory (building number 606) in 1965 as an alert crew quarters for the Post Attack Command Control System (PACCS) to support their Boeing KC-135A Auxiliary Airborne Command Post (AACP). SAC used this aircraft to maintain an alternate nuclear launch capability for its bomber and ICBM force in case of all out nuclear war with the Soviet Union and ground command facilities and SAC command and control facilities were knocked out of commission from a Russian nuclear strike. The base also remodeled two former 54th FIS alert support structures (building numbers 608 and 609). This alert grouping for the 54th FIS was one of the first in the United States to maintain Cold War deterrence. Its readiness/maintenance hangars were reused WWII hangars already at Ellsworth (building numbers 601 and 605). These 1942 hangars were similar to those used on other Air Force bases as the Department of Defense rushed to implement Cold War deterrence against the possibility of Russian long-range bomber attack. The hangars are 120 feet long and 96 feet wide, with panel sliding doors along their 120-ft. front facing apron. Heater room space and office space was provided by a lean-to on the side opposite the hangar doors. Heat for the hangars was provided by a hot air furnace stocker fed with automatic control. Heat for the office space was provided by an upright steam boiler and radiation system. One of these world war hangars remains standing at Ellsworth AFB. Its functions have constantly changed from WWII to the present. There is a plaque inside the hangar honoring those who previously served with the 54th FIS.[1]

Convair F-102 Delta Dagger
Air Defense Command wanted to maintain its air defense responsibility over US airspace and planned to convert its fighter interceptor squadrons from the F-89J to the Convair supersonic F-102 Delta Dagger, an interim delta-interceptor design fielded by the Air Force until the arrival of the more capable/supersonic Convair F-106 Delta Dart. The 54th FIS prepared to transition from the F-89J to the F-102,

with the alert hangar modified for the new aircraft, simulator for the new and alert pilots scheduled for training in the new single-seat interceptor.

The Convair F-102A Delta Dagger was the first supersonic Air Force fighter configured with a delta-wing. It was designed to protect the Continental United States against over the north pole Russian Air Force bombers, especially the supersonic Tupolev Tu-22 Blinder, capable of a maximum speed of Mach 1.4, with a service ceiling of 59,000 feet. Its drawback was that it had a short range of 1,400 miles, but could be air refueled, as SAC's Boeing B-52s, for unlimited range.

The F-102A's design created a wasp-waist fuselage shape with delta wings and tail to become one of the Air Force's hottest interceptor. The aircraft was not armed with guns but rockets/missiles, including the Falcon air-to-air missile armed to an atomic warhead, replacing the F-89J's Genie air to air missile.

Specifications and Performance Information

Manufacturer	Convair Aircraft
Type	Single-seat interceptor
Wingspan	38 feet 1-inch
Length	68 feet 4 1/2-inches
Tail height	21 feet 2 1/2-inches
Tread width	14 feet 6-inches
Power plant	(one) 11,700 pound thrust Pratt & Whitney J57-P-23 turbojet
With afterburner	17,200 pound thrust
Maximum speed	825 mph
Combat radius	840 miles
Maximum range	1,350 miles
Empty weight	19,903 pounds
With external tanks	20,234 pounds
Usable fuel	7,053 pounds
With external tanks	9,848 pounds
Armament	1,194 pounds
Clean total weight	28,150 pounds
With external tanks	31,270 pounds
Maximum weight	31,500 pounds
Armament(s)	(24) 70 mm folding-fin unguided rockets Standard(3) Falcon heat seeking air to air missiles with conventional high explosive warhead
War fighting	(one) Falcon, nuclear .25 (nuclear) Kiloton warhead, heat seeking air to air missile.

Appendix F

Electronics	Hughes MG-1C Fire Control
Intercept profile	Once onboard electronic equipment located the hostile airborne target, the radar guided the aircraft into missile launch position. With the electronic fire control automatically fires the air to air missiles.
Operational service	1960 to 1970
Number built	875[2]

The South Dakota Air and Space Museum acquired F-102A, aircraft serial number 56-1017 from storage at Holloman AFB, New Mexico, in July 1987. A team from Ellsworth AFB loaded the aircraft on two flatbed trailers, taking eleven days for transportation preparation by the 28th Bomb Wing Maintenance Squadron and two days for travel, arriving at Ellsworth AFB for restoration. It was not finally restored until August 16, 2014.[3] The historic aircraft was painted to reflect its significant heritage of service with the Air Force and moved to the museum grounds in May 2015, where it will be permanently displayed.[4]

Convair F-102A Delta Dagger on display at the Ellsworth AFB flight line during the 28th Bomb Wing's "Community Appreciate Day," August 16, 2014. The delta wing fighter was restored by volunteers from the South Dakota Air and Space Museum. The aircraft is now on display on museum grounds (2015). *Author Photo*

APPENDIX G

A Few Remaining Northrop F-89 Scorpions

F-89J (serial number 54-0298) on display at Dyess AFB Air Park, Texas. *Author Photo*

F-89J (serial number 52-1927) on display at the Castle Air Force Museum Airpark (Castle AFB is no longer an active installation), Atwater, California. *Author Photo*

Appendix G

F-89J (serial number 52-1941) on display at the Peterson Air and Space Museum, Peterson AFB, Colorado. *Author Photo*

F-89J (serial number 53-2547) on display at Great Falls Air National Guard Airpark, Great Falls International Airport, Montana. This aircraft fired the only nuclear armed Genie on July 19, 1957, during Operation Plumbbob for "Shot John," detonating a 1.5 kiloton warhead at 18,000 feet, within 11,000 feet of the escaping F-89J. *Montana Air National Guard*

F-89J (53-2674) on display at the Pima Air and Space Museum, Tucson, Arizona. *Author Photo*

F-89J (serial number 53-1949) on display at March Field Air Museum (March AFB is no longer an active Air Force installation). *Author Photo*

APPENDIX H

The End of Cold War Warriors F-89Js at the "Bone Yard"

The 309th Aerospace Maintenance and Regeneration Group, US Air Material Command, Tucson, Arizona

The Aerospace Maintenance and Regeneration Center is a joint service facility managed by the United States Air Force Material Command. It has earned the nickname the "Bone Yard," which is an aerospace storage and maintenance facility adjacent to Davis-Monthan AFB, providing a service to all branches of the United State military branches, as well as other national agencies. As of June 2015, the large facility controls an inventory of over 4,200 aircraft, including many other categories of military equipment. The center works hard promoting itself as more than a "Bone Yard," since it returns more money in equipment than it costs each year to operate. Many of the stored aircraft can be returned to operational status in a short period of time and there is a continuous process of anti-corrosion and re-preservation work that keeps the aircraft in stable condition during storage at the center. The center reclaims spare parts and eventual disposal of airframes no longer deemed viable for military service. After seventeen years of active and reserve operation F-89Js were flown to the center. Some were given to museums and others were eventually melted into metal ingots, or sold as scrap metal for recycling and manufacturing into new items.[1]

F-89J on the ramp at Davis Monthan AFB, Arizona, prior to being towed to the 309th Aerospace Vehicle Storage and Regeneration Group (AMARG) for storage, equipment removal, and scrapping. The F-89Js went from active duty to Air National Guard and Air Force Reserve wings/squadrons prior to being flown to Davis Monthan AFB and on to AMARG. Two F-89Js parked on the aircraft ramp. *This and subsequent photos of F-89Js: Davis Monthan AFB, Air Force Material Command, 309th Aerospace Vehicle Storage and Regeneration Group June 26, 2015*

The 54th Fighter-Interceptor Squadron

Once the F-89Js were at the AMARG facility usable equipment was removed. These F-89Js have had their engine access panels removed. This aircraft came from the Montana Air National Guard.

Completely processed F-89J placed in the desert in outdoor storage (low humidity excellent for storage of aircraft pending disposition) at AMARG. Engine intakes and exhausts are sealed, the fuel has been removed, and preventive lubricants have been added to the aircraft's system. External skin openings into the fuselage are closed and sealed, as well as the cockpit.

Appendix H

Close-up view of rows of F-89Js in storage at AMARG.

The 54th Fighter-Interceptor Squadron

At various times AMARG parked newly arrived aircraft along a perimeter road for viewing by visitors to the aircraft storage facility. In the foreground is a F-89J Scorpion. Continuing down the parked row of aircraft is a Lockheed F-89 Starfire, Republic F-84F Thunderflash, and in the background rows of Boeing B-47 Stratojet bombers.

Appendix H

GLOSSARY

Abort: Aircraft trouble.

Air Defense: Defense against attack on an air defense area by airborne aircraft or guided missiles. The sum total of all measures undertaken for this purpose. An organization or activity providing this defense.

Air Defense Area (ADA): A specifically defined extensive area that includes the objective of possible enemy air attack and for which air defense is, or must, be provided.

Air Defense Command (ADC): The command providing air defense for the United States Air Force for the air defense of the United States.

Air Defense Control Center (ADCC): A land-based, air operations installation that with early warning installations, air defense direction centers, and other organizations and facilities provides air control and warning, and control and direction of active air defense in a given Air Defense Area.

Air Defense Controller: An aircraft controller responsible for controlling and vectoring friendly aircraft during air defense and coordinating the operations of anti-aircraft artillery.

Air Defense Direction Center: A ground control intercept station that controls interceptors and anti-aircraft fire and reports the progress of air defense to the Air Defense Control Center.

Air Defense Identification Zone (ADIZ): The airspace above a specific geographical area in which the control and ready recognition of aircraft is required.

Air Defense Operation: An air operation concerned with the air defense of an area.

Air Defense Sector: Each Air Defense Sector is divided into Air Defense Sub-sectors and is provided with an Air Division and an Aircraft Control and Warning Group.

Applejack: The Red Alert, one of the various stages.

Bumpheads: Two 54th fighters make practice runs on each other.

Burythedot: Center the target.

Fadeout: The exercise is over.

Fanout: Spreading the alert: one man calls two, two calls four, four calls eight, etc.

Lemon Juice: Yellow Alert.

Rollerskate: The radar station at Ellsworth AFB.

Snowman: Relax—the time to a possible take-off will now be long enough to permit a cup of coffee.

Splash: Knock the target from the sky.

Turnaround: The time required to service a plane and have it ready to fly again.

NOTES

Introduction
1. Robert O'Daniel, Rapid City, South Dakota, to author, May 15, 2012. Robert O'Daniel was born in 1933, in Redfield, South Dakota. He graduated from Rapid City High School on May 1, 1952. He joined the US Navy on November 7, 1952, with the rank yeoman, third class. Upon his discharge from the Navy on September 17, 1956, he joined the US Air Force, trained as a flight records/administrative clerk, and was assigned to the 54th FIS, Ellsworth AFB, South Dakota. In 1959, as chief clerk of the wing administration section, he maintained publication files; prepared correspondence, reports, and messages; maintained suspense files; and assigned tasks to personnel under him commensurate with their capabilities. In December 1959, he was assigned to the 731st Radar Squadron at Sundance AFS, Wyoming, as a staff sergeant (NCOIC) of the administrative section. He was later assigned to Detachment 2, Headquarters 71st Surveillance Wing with Air Defense Command at Clear BMEWS, Alaska, on June 13, 1962. He was then assigned to Headquarters, Pacific Air Forces, Hickam AFB, Hawaii. He had temporary duty assignment to Wake Island, earning a "letter of commendation" for his assistance in handling South Vietnamese refugees as part of Operation New Life while assigned to the 15th Operations Squadron. He retired from the Air Force on April 1, 1977, as a master sergeant.

History of the 54th FIS
1. "History of the 54th Fighter Interceptor Squadron." Records retrieved by Administrative Clerk MSgt. Robert O'Daniel after the squadron was discontinued and sent to author.
2. "History of the 54th Fighter-Interceptor Squadron." Records retrieved by MSgt. Robert O'Daniel.
3. Robert C. Mikesh, *Japan's World War II Balloon Bomb Attacks on North America* (Washington, DC: National Air and Space, Smithsonian Institution Press, 1973), 1.
4. "History of the 54th Fighter-Interceptor Squadron."
5. "Commander brings in first of new jets for local base," the *Rapid City Journal*, Rapid City, South Dakota, January 22, 1954.
6. "History of the 54th Fighter-Interceptor Squadron."

7. "F-86D's arrive, Col. Benedict brings in first one from California in two hours," *Recon Observer*, Ellsworth Air Force Base, 28th Bomb Wing, Rapid City, South Dakota, January 29, 1954.
8. "History of the 54th Fighter-Interceptor-Squadron."
9. "Jets Buzz' only for real alert," *The Recon Observer*, Ellsworth Air Fore Base Public Affairs.
10. "The History of the 54th Fighter-Interceptor Squadron."
11. "Ellsworth pilot bails from jet," *The Rapid City Journal*, Rapid City, South Dakota, June 12, 1954. Via press release from North Dakota through the Associated Press release.
12. "History of 54th Fighter-Interceptor Squadron," Ellsworth Air Force Base Public Affairs.
13. "Jet piloted commended on landing," *The Rapid City Journal*, Rapid City, South Dakota, July 13, 1959.
14. "History of 54th Fighter-Interceptor Squadron," Ellsworth Air Force Base Public Affairs.
15. "54th returns to EAFB after 30 days of training," *The Rapid City Journal*, Rapid City, South Dakota, November 7, 1954.
16. "History of 54th Fighter-Interceptor Squadron," Ellsworth Air Force Base Public Affairs.
17. "Crashes kill two EAFB Airmen, Sabre Jet, copter fall on prairie," *The Rapid City Journal*, Rapid City, South Dakota, February 18, 1966.
18. "Warning!-Two lethal rockets missing from jet," *The Rapid City Journal*, Rapid City, South Dakota, February 23, 1955.
19 "Missing rocket located," *The Rapid City Journal*, Rapid City, South Dakota, March 7, 1955.
20. "Anniversary of Air Defense unit noted," *The Rapid City Daily Journal*, Rapid City, South Dakota, March 1, 1955.
21. "History of 54th Fighter-Interceptor Squadron," Ellsworth Air Force Base Public Affairs.
22. "Airmen of 54th to live better," *The Rapid City Daily Journal*, Rapid City, South Dakota, June 4, 1955.
23. "54th FIS alert hangar undergo improvements," *The Rapid City Journal*, Rapid City, South Dakota, June 10, 1955.
24. "History of 54th Fighter-Interceptor Squadron," Ellsworth Air Force Base Public Affairs.
25. "We'll come out on top, 54th, 29th Fighter Squadrons set to go after spot on CDAF Team." *The Rapid City Journal,* Rapid City, South Dakota, June 29, 1955.
26. "History of 54th Fighter-Interceptor Squadron," Ellsworth Air Force Base Public Affairs.

27. "Base jet pilot killed in crash," *The Rapid City Daily Journal*, Rapid City, South Dakota, July 13, 1955.
28. "Skidding in at 150 mph," *The Rapid City Journal*, Rapid City, South Dakota, October 27, 1955.
29. "Airmen donate rare type blood; 54th flies it to Huron, South Dakota," *The Black Hills Bomber*, Rapid City, South Dakota, November 16, 1955.
30. "History of 54th Fighter-Interceptor Squadron," Ellsworth Air Force Base Public Affairs.
31. "Rocket training pays hit dividend to 54th," *Air Force Times*, Springfield, Virginia, March 17, 1956.
32. "54th FIS wraps-up division rocket meet with clutch hits, 'sudden death' shoot-off, Norris top man on team, Hardin, Hull high for 29th," *The Monitor, 29th Air Division (Defense),* Malmstrom Air Force Base, Montana, June 1956.
33. "History of 54th Fighter-Interceptor Squadron," Ellsworth Air Force Base Public Affairs.
34. "Fighter Pilot bails to safety, jet sets fire in Rapid South Dakota, October 4, 1956.
35. "History of 54th Fighter-Interceptor Squadron," Ellsworth Air Force Base Public Affairs.
36. "EAFB pilots take part on atomic tests," *The Rapid City Journal*, Rapid City, South Dakota, July 28, 1957.
37. "History of atomic cloud sampling," *Atomic Energy Commission Technical Library, SWEH-2- 0034,* dated January 1963, Air Force Weapons Library (declassified August 5 1957).
38. "Unique team to inspect 54th Fighter Squadron," *The Black Hills Bomber*, Rapid City, South Dakota, August 8, 1957.
39. "History of 54th Fighter-Interceptor Squadron," Ellsworth Air Force Base Public Affairs.
40. Letter from Headquarters Air Defense Command to Commander 54th Fighter-Interceptor Squadron, Ellsworth Air Force Base, South Dakota, dated November 1, 1957.
41. "Historical Record of the 54th Fighter Interceptor Squadron, Ellsworth Air Force Base, South Dakota, for the period ending 30 June 1958." Ellsworth Air Force Base, South Dakota, 54th Fighter Interceptor Squadron, declassified, November 20, 1978." Montgomery, Alabama: Maxwell Air Force Base, Air Force Historical Research Agency (Tammy T. Horton, CD/Microfilm Department) to author, June 16, 2015.
42. "History of 54th Fighter-Interceptor Squadron," Ellsworth Air Force Base Public Affairs.
43. "Defense concept explained," *The Rapid City Journal*, Rapid City, South Dakota, May 17, 1958.

44. "54th FIS picnic at Canyon Lake Park," *The Rapid City Journal*, Rapid City, South Dakota, June 13, 1958.
45. "History of 54th Fighter-Interceptor Squadron," Ellsworth Air Force Base Public Affairs.
46. Headquarters Central Air Defense Force, "Redeployment of 54th Fighter-Interceptor Squadron," Malmstrom Air Force Base, Montana, 29 July 1958. Harold L. Neely, Brigadier General, USAF, Commander, Central Air Defense Force, 29th Air Division.
47. "History of 54th Fighter-Interceptor Squadron," Ellsworth Air Force Base Public Affairs.
48. "Historical Record of the 54th Fighter Interceptor Squadron, Ellsworth Air Force Base, South Dakota, for the period ending 30 September 1958." Ellsworth Air Force Base, South Dakota, 54th Fighter Interceptor Squadron, declassified, November 20, 1978." Montgomery, Alabama: Maxwell Air Force Base, Air Force Historical Research Agency (Tammy T. Horton, CD/Microfilm Department) to author, June 16, 2015.
49. "History of 54th Fighter-Interceptor Squadron," Ellsworth Air Force Base Public Affairs.
50. "Historical Record of the 54th Fighter-Interceptor Squadron, Ellsworth Air Force Base, South Dakota, for the period ending 31 December 1958."
51. "It's all in a day's flying with the 54th Fighter- Interceptor Squadron," *The Black Hills Bomber*, Ellsworth Air Force Base, 28th Bomb Wing Public Affairs, November 14, 1958.
52. "History of 54th Fighter-Interceptor Squadron," Ellsworth Air Force Base Public Affairs.
53. Harold L. Neely, Brigadier General, USAF, Commander, Headquarters 29th Air Division (Defense) (ADC), United States Air Force, Malmstrom Air Force Base, Montana, "Commendation," to Commander, 54th Fighter- Interceptor Squadron, Ellsworth Air Force Base, South Dakota, 15 December 1958.
54. 54th Fighter-Interceptor Squadron breaks 28 global records for ADC *The Black Hills Bomber*, Ellsworth Air Force base, 28th Bomb Wing, Public Affairs, January 16, 1959.
55. Headquarters Central Air Defense Force (ADC), United States Air Force, Richards-Gebaur Air Force Base, Missouri, General Order Number 7, "Central Air Defense Force "A" Award," dated January 30, 1959.
56. Headquarters Air Defense Command, "Citation to accompany the Central Air Defense 'A' Award to the 54th Fighter-Interceptor Squadron," Ent Air Force Base, Colorado Springs, Colorado: United States Air Force, January 30, 1959.
57. Headquarters 29th Air Division (Defense), "Organization-Field, Organization and Function's Fighter-Interceptor Squadrons," *29AD Manual, No. 23-1*, Malmstrom Air Force Base, Montana, June 1, 1959.

58. "Historical Record of the 54th Fighter Interceptor Squadron, Ellsworth Air Force Base, South Dakota, for the period ending 31 March 1958." Ellsworth Air Force Base, South Dakota, 54th Fighter Interceptor Squadron, declassified, November 20, 1978." Montgomery, Alabama: Maxwell Air Force Base, Air Force Historical Research Agency (Tammy T. Horton, CD/Microfilm Department) to author, June 16, 2015.
59. "History of 54th Fighter-Interceptor Squadron," Ellsworth Air Force Base Public Affairs.
60. "Historical Record of the 54th Fighter Interceptor Squadron, Ellsworth Air Force Base, South Dakota, for the period ending 30 June 1959." Ellsworth Air Force Base, South Dakota, 54th Fighter Interceptor Squadron, declassified, November 20, 1978." Montgomery, Alabama: Maxwell Air Force Base, Air Force Historical Research Agency (Tammy T. Horton, CD/Microfilm Department) to author, June 16, 2015.
61. "History of 54th Fighter-Interceptor Squadron," Ellsworth Air Force Base Public Affairs.
62. "History of the 54th Fighter-Interceptor Squadron. MSgt. Robert O'Daniel.
63. "History of 54th Fighter-Interceptor Squadron," Ellsworth Air Force Base Public Affairs.
64. 54th Fighter-Interceptor Squadron, "54th FIS using MG-12 system shatters 28 records in nation-wide ADC contest," Ellsworth Air Force Base, 54th FIS Field Engineering Department, South Dakota, August 20, 1959.
65. "54th FIS returns from Arizona competition with 28 world records," *The Rapid City Journal*, Rapid City, South Dakota, August 20, 1959.
66. "54th Fighter Squadron named Nation's best," *The Rapid City Journal*, Rapid City, South Dakota, September 1, 1959.
67. "Ellsworth FIS visits RGAFB," Continental Air Defense Force Public Service (Affairs) to *The Rapid City Journal*, Rapid City, South Dakota, September 15, 1959.
68. "54th Fighter-Interceptor Squadron to be feted at Hughes Award Banquet," typed sheet from Administration Section, 54th FIS, posted on Squadron Bulletin Board, via MSgt. Robert P. O'Daniel, USAF (Ret.) to author.
69. "History of 54th Fighter-Interceptor Squadron," Ellsworth Air Force Base Public Affairs.
70. "Historical Record of the 54th Fighter Interceptor Squadron, Ellsworth Air Force Base, South Dakota, for the period ending 31 December 1959." Ellsworth Air Force Base, South Dakota, 54th Fighter Interceptor Squadron, declassified, November 20, 1978." Montgomery, Alabama: Maxwell Air Force Base, Air Force Historical Research Agency (Tammy T. Horton, CD/Microfilm Department) to author, June 16, 2015.

71. "History of 54th Fighter-Interceptor Squadron," Ellsworth Air Force Base Public Affairs.
72. "Historical Record of the 54th Fighter Interceptor Squadron, Ellsworth Air Force Base, South Dakota, for the period ending 31 December 1959." Ellsworth Air Force Base, South Dakota, 54th Fighter Interceptor Squadron, declassified, November 20, 1978." Montgomery, Alabama: Maxwell Air Force Base, Air Force Historical Research Agency (Tammy T. Horton, CD/Microfilm Department) to author, June 16, 2015.
73. "Practice alerts routine for 54th," *The Rapid City Journal*, Rapid City, South Dakota, October 4, 1959.
74. Earl F. Bunner, TSgt., USAF, NCOIC Flight Simulator, "Historical program, Flight Simulator," Ellsworth Air Force Base, South Dakota, 54th Fighter-Interceptor Squadron, May 3, 1960.
75. "54th Fighter-Interceptor Squadron, "Historical record of the 54th Fighter-Interceptor Squadron (ADC), for the period ending June 30, 1960," Ellsworth Air Force Base, July 1960.
76. 414st Strategic Wing, "Operations and Support Plan for redeployment 54th Fighter-Interceptor Squadron (ADC)," Glasgow Air Force Base, Montana, June 1, 1960.
77. "An empty alert hangar and ...The 54th FIS goes TDY," *The 29th Air Division Monitor*, Malmstrom Air Force Base, Montana, July 15, 1960.
78. 414st Strategic Wing, "Operations and Support Plan for redeployment 54th Fighter-Interceptor Squadron (ADC)," Glasgow Air Force Base, Montana, June 1, 1960.
79. "Historical Record of the 54th Fighter Interceptor Squadron, Ellsworth Air Force Base, South Dakota, for the period ending 30 September 1960." Ellsworth Air Force Base, South Dakota, 54th Fighter Interceptor Squadron, declassified, November 20, 1978." Montgomery, Alabama: Maxwell Air Force Base, Air Force Historical Research Agency (Tammy T. Horton, CD/Microfilm Department) to author, June 16, 2015.
80. "The 54th was a good outfit," *The Rapid City Journal*, Rapid City, South Dakota, August 28, 1960.

81. "Ellsworth to lose the 54th Fighter Sqdn," *The Rapid City Journal*, Rapid City, South Dakota, September 14, 1960.
82. 731st Radar Squadron, "A guide to Sundance Air Force Station Wyoming," Sundance, Wyoming: Marvin C. Hamilton, Major, USAF, Commander, 731st Radar Squadron, Air Defense Command, September 19, 1960.
83. MSgt. Robert O'Daniel, Rapid City, South Dakota, to author, May 1, 2012.
84. "Air Force ends nuclear power unit airlift," *Sundance Times*, Sundance, Wyoming, May 1961.
85. "Ceremony opens Containment Area at Radar Station," *The Rapid City Journal*, Rapid City, South Dakota, May 10, 1961.
86. "AF's first atomic power plant begins operation at Sundance," *The Rapid City Journal*, Rapid City, South Dakota, September 1962.
87. "Sundance recalls nuclear reactor," *Sundance Times*, Sundance, Wyoming, May 1990.
88. Headquarters 29th Air Division (SAGE) (ADC), "Extension of Discontinuance Date of 54 FIS," Malmstrom Air Force Base, Montana: United States Air Force, September 22, 1960.
89. Paul Ranney, Chairman, Military Affairs Committee, Rapid City Chamber of Commerce, to Lt. Col. Ernest D. Nuckols, Commander, 54th Fighter-Interceptor Squadron, Ellsworth Air Force Base, South Dakota, November 1, 1960.
90. Headquarters Air Defense Command, "Discontinuance of Units," Colorado Springs, Colorado: United States Air Force, Ent Air Force Base, General Order Number 140, September 22, 1960.

Epilogue
1. "The 54th was a good outfit," Rapid City, South Dakota: *The Rapid City Journal*, Rapid City, South Dakota, editorial, Sunday, August 28, 1960.
2. "F-89J, Serial Number 53-2453," Montgomery, Alabama: Maxwell Air Force Base, Air Force Historical Research Center.
3. "54th Fighter Squadron," http://www.afhra.af.mil/factsheets/factsheet.asp?id=10270.

Appendices
Appendix A:
1. "Curtiss P-36A Hawk," specifications and performance information, Dayton, Ohio: Wright Patterson Air Force Base, National Museum of the United States Air Force, "World War II Gallery."
2. "Curtiss P-40E Warhawk," specifications and performance information, Dayton, Ohio: Wright Patterson Air Force Base, National Museum of the United States Air Force, "World War II Gallery."
3. "Curtiss P-43 Lancer," specifications and performance information, Dayton, Ohio: Wright Patterson Air Force Base, National Museum of the United States Air Force, "World War II Gallery."
4. "Lockheed P-38 Lightning," specifications and performance information, Dayton, Ohio: Wright Patterson Air Force Base, National Museum of the United States Air Force, "World War II Gallery."
5. "North American P-51 Mustang," specifications and performance information, Dayton, Ohio: Wright Patterson Air Force Base, National Museum of the United States Air Force, "World War II Gallery."
6. "Republic F-84E," specifications and performance information, Dayton, Ohio: Wright Patterson Air Force Base, National Museum of the United States Air Force, "Cold War Gallery."
7. "North American F-86D Sabre Dog," specifications and performance information, Dayton, Ohio: Wright Patterson Air Force Base, National Museum of the United States Air Force, "Cold War Gallery."
8. "Northrop J-89J Scorpion," specifications and performance information, Dayton, Ohio: Wright Patterson Air Force Base, National Museum of the United States Air Force, "Cold War Gallery."
9. "F-15 Eagle," *US Air Force Fact Sheet,* Dayton, Ohio: Wright Patterson Air Force Base, National Museum of the United States Air Force, "Cold War Gallery."

Appendix B:
1. "Hughes AIM-4 Falcon," Dayton, Ohio: Wright Patterson Air Force Base, National Museum of the United State Air Force, "Cold War Gallery."
2. "McDonnell-Douglas AIR-2A Genie Rocket," Dayton, Ohio: Wright-Patterson Air Force Base, National Museum of the United States Air Force, "Cold War Gallery."
3. Lt. Col. George A. Larson, USAF (Ret.), *Thunder Over Dakota, The Complete History of Ellsworth Air Force Base, South Dakota,* Chapter Six, "Nike Ajax and Nike Hercules," Atglen, PA.: Schiffer Publishing, Ltd., 2013.

4. "Nike-Ajax surface-to-air missile," Dayton, Ohio: Wright-Patterson Air Force Base, National Museum of the United States Air Force, "Cold War Gallery."
5. The Nike Historical Society, "Hercules MIM-14, MIM-14A, MIM-14B," (http://nikemissile.org/IFC/nike_hercules.shtml).

Appendix C:
1. "54th Fighter-Interceptor Squadron Commanders," Ent Air Force Base, Colorado Springs, Colorado: United States Air Force, Air Defense Command, September 19, 1960. "Historical Record of the period ending September 30, 1960." Note: end date of the 54th FIS added by author.

Appendix D:
1. 4950th Test Group, "Operation Plumbbob, August 9, 1957 through October 7, 1957," Folder: History of Cloud Sampling. Kirkland Air Force Base, New Mexico, Air Force Special Weapons Center, Technical Library. Declassified August 20, 1986.

Appendix E:
1. "AF probes fatal F-51 Crash," *The Rapid City Journal,* Rapid City, South Dakota, November 16, 1951.
2. "Pilot killed in crash of air base jet," *The Rapid City Journal,* Rapid City, South Dakota, June 11, 1953.
3. "Captain dies instantly in base jet crash, wreckage found near Faith after four-hour search," *The Rapid City Journal,* Rapid City, South Dakota, June 23, 1953.
4. "Sabre jet 'copter fall on prairie," *The Rapid City Journal,* Rapid City, South Dakota, February 18, 1955.

Appendix F:
1. "History of South Dakota Air and Space Museum," South Dakota Air and Space Museum, historical archives to author.
2. "Convair F-102A Delta Dagger," Dayton, Ohio: Wright Patterson Air Force Base, National Museum of the United States Air Force, "Cold War Gallery."
3. "Museum acquires F-102 aircraft for display," *Plainsman,* Ellsworth Air Force Base, 28th Bomb Wing Public Affairs, July 21, 1987.
4. "Ellsworth Hosts Community Appreciation Day, F-102 Delta Dagger," *The Patriot,* Ellsworth Air Force Base, 28th Bomb Wing Public Affairs, August 8, 2014.

Appendix G:
1. "Museum acquires F-102 aircraft for display," Plainsman, Ellsworth Air Force Base, 28th Bomb Wing Public Affairs, July 21, 1987.
2. "Ellsworth Hosts Community Appreciation Day, F-102 Delta Dagger," *The Patriot*, Ellsworth Air Force Base, 28th Bomb Wing Public Affairs, August 8, 2014.

Appendix H:
1. "What is AMARG?" 309th Aerospace Maintenance and Regeneration Group, Administration to author June 12, 2015. Also available at http://www/amarcexperience.com.

SOURCES

"ADC—Detection and Defense." *Air Force Almanac*, 1972. Washington, DC, Air Force Association, 1972.

"Construction and operation of ammunition magazine area." College Park, Maryland: National Archives and Records Administration II, Record Group 156, Office of the Chief of Ordnance, 1954. Courtesy US Senator Tim Johnson (South Dakota) to author, June 1, 2013.

"Convair F-102A Delta Dagger." Dayton, Ohio: Wright Patterson Air Force Base, National Museum of the United States Air Force, "Cold War Gallery."

"Curtiss P-36A Hawk," specifications and performance information. Dayton, Ohio: Wright Patterson Air Force Base, National Museum of the United States Air Force, "World War II Gallery."

"Curtiss P-40E Warhawk," specifications and performance information. Dayton, Ohio: Wright Patterson Air Force Base, National Museum of the United States Air Force, "World War II Gallery."

"Curtiss P-43 Lancer," specifications and performance information. Dayton, Ohio: Wright Patterson Air Force Base, National Museum of the United States Air Force, "World War II Gallery."

Ellsworth Air Force Base Fact Sheet. South Dakota: Ellsworth Air Force Base, 28th Bomb Wing Public Affairs.

Environmental Protection Agency. National Oil and Hazardous Substances Pollution Contingency Plan; National Priorities List; "Notice of intent for partial deletion of the Ellsworth Air Force Base Site from the National Priorities List," Washington, DC: June 8, 2006.

"Exposé of Soviet Espionage, May 1960." Washington, D.C.: Federal Bureau of Investigation, United States Department of Justice. John Edgar Hoover, Director of the Federal Bureau of Investigation. Prepared for transmittal to the President of the United States (Dwight D. Eisenhower), May 23, 1960.

"F-89J, Serial Number 53-2453." Montgomery, Alabama: Maxwell Air Force Base, Air Force Historical Research Center.

54th Fighter-Interceptor Squadron. "54th FIS using MG-12 system shatters 28 records in nation-wide ADC contest." Ellsworth Air Force Base, 54th FIS Field Engineering Department, South Dakota, August 20, 1959.

"54th Fighter-Interceptor Squadron Commanders." Ent Air Force Base, Colorado Springs, Colorado: United States Air Force, Air Defense Command, September 19, 1960.

54th Fighter-Interceptor Squadron. "Historical Record of the period ending September 30, 1960." Note: end date of the 54th FIS added by author.

54th Fighter-Interceptor Squadron. "Historical record of the 54th Fighter-Interceptor Squadron (ADC), for the period ending June 30, 1960." Ellsworth Air Force Base, July 1960.

54th Fighter-Interceptor Squadron. "Historical Record of the 54th Fighter-Interceptor Squadron (ADC) for the period ending September 20, 1960." Ellsworth Air Force Base, Rapid City, South Dakota, September 30, 1960.

"54th Fighter-Interceptor Squadron to be feted at Hughes Award Banquet." Typed sheet from Administration Section, 54th FIS, posted on Squadron Bulletin Board, via MSgt. Robert P. O'Daniel, USAF (Ret.) to Lt. Col. George A. Larson, USAF (Ret.)

414st Strategic Wing. "Operations and Support Plan for redeployment 54th Fighter-Interceptor Squadron (ADC)." Glasgow Air Force Base, Montana, June 1, 1960.

4950th Test Group, "Operation Plumbbob, August 9, 1957 through October 7, 1957," Folder: History of Cloud Sampling. Kirkland Air Force Base, New Mexico, Air Force Special Weapons Center, Technical Library. Declassified August 20, 1986.

Gunston, Bill. *Jane's Fighting Aircraft of World War II*. New York: Crescent Books, 1994.

Hanson, Chuck. *US Nuclear Weapons, The Secret Story*. Arlington, Texas: Aerofax, 1988.

Headquarters Air Defense Command. "Citation to accompany the Central Air Defense 'A' Award to the 54th Fighter-Interceptor Squadron." Ent Air Force Base, Colorado Springs, Colorado: United States Air Force, January 30, 1959.

Headquarters Air Defense Command. "Discontinuance of Units." Colorado Springs, Colorado: United States Air Force, Ent Air Force Base, General Order Number 140, September 22, 1960.

Headquarters Central Air Defense Force. "Redeployment of 54th Fighter-Interceptor Squadron." Malmstrom Air Force Base, Montana, July 29, 1958. Harold L. Neely, Brigadier General, USAF, Commander, Central Air Defense Force, 29th Air Division.

Headquarters Central Air Defense Force (ADC), United States Air Force, Richards-Gebaur Air Force Base, Missouri, General Order Number 7, "Central Air Defense Force 'A' Award," dated January 30, 1959.

Headquarters 29th Air Division (SAGE) (ADC). "Extension of Discontinuance Date of 54 FIS," Malmstrom Air Force Base, Montana: United States Air Force, September 22, 1960.

Headquarters 29th Air Division (Defense). "Organization-Field, Organization and Function's Fighter-Interceptor Squadrons," 29AD Manual, No. 23-1, Malmstrom Air Force Base, Montana, June1, 1959.

Heflen, Woodford Agee, ed. *The United States Air Force Dictionary*. Montgomery, Alabama.: Maxwell Air Force Base, Air University Press, 1956.

"Historical Record of the 54th Fighter Interceptor Squadron, Ellsworth Air Force Base, South Dakota, for the period ending 30 June 1958." Ellsworth Air Force Base, South Dakota, 54rth Fighter Interceptor Squadron, declassified, November 20, 1978." Montgomery, Alabama: Maxwell Air Force Base, Air Force Historical Research Agency (Tammy T. Horton, CD/Microfilm Department) to author, June 16, 2015.

"Historical Record of the 54th Fighter Interceptor Squadron, Ellsworth Air Force Base, South Dakota, for the period ending 30 September 1958." Ellsworth Air Force Base, South Dakota, 54th Fighter Interceptor Squadron, declassified, November 20, 1978. Montgomery, Alabama: Maxwell Air Force Base, Air Force Historical Research Agency (Tammy T. Horton, CD/Microfilm Department) to author, June 16, 2015.

"Historical Record of the 54th Fighter Interceptor Squadron, Ellsworth Air Force Base, South Dakota, for the period ending 31 December 1958." Ellsworth Air Force Base, South Dakota, 54th Fighter Interceptor Squadron, declassified, November 20, 1978. Montgomery, Alabama: Maxwell Air Force Base, Air Force Historical Research Agency (Tammy T. Horton, CD/Microfilm Department) to author, June 16, 2015.

"Historical Record of the 54th Fighter Interceptor Squadron, Ellsworth Air Force Base, South Dakota, for the period ending 31 March 1958." Ellsworth Air Force Base, South Dakota, 54th Fighter Interceptor Squadron, declassified, November 20, 1978. Montgomery, Alabama: Maxwell Air Force Base, Air Force Historical Research Agency (Tammy T. Horton, CD/Microfilm Department) to author, June 16, 2015.

"Historical Record of the 54th Fighter Interceptor Squadron, Ellsworth Air Force Base, South Dakota, for the period ending 30 June 1959." Ellsworth Air Force Base, South Dakota, 54th Fighter Interceptor Squadron, declassified, November 20, 1978. Montgomery, Alabama: Maxwell Air Force Base, Air Force Historical Research Agency (Tammy T. Horton, CD/Microfilm Department) to author, June 16, 2015.

"Historical Record of the 54th Fighter Interceptor Squadron, Ellsworth Air Force Base, South Dakota, for the period ending 30 September 1959." Ellsworth Air Force Base, South Dakota, 54th Fighter Interceptor Squadron, declassified, November 20, 1978. Montgomery, Alabama: Maxwell Air Force Base, Air Force Historical Research Agency (Tammy T. Horton, CD/Microfilm Department) to author, June 16, 2015.

"Historical Record of the 54th Fighter Interceptor Squadron, Ellsworth Air Force Base, South Dakota, for the period ending 31 December 1959." Ellsworth Air Force Base, South Dakota, 54th Fighter Interceptor Squadron, declassified,

November 20, 1978. Montgomery, Alabama: Maxwell Air Force Base, Air Force Historical Research Agency (Tammy T. Horton, CD/Microfilm Department) to author, June 16, 2015.

"Historical Record of the 54th Fighter Interceptor Squadron, Ellsworth Air Force Base, South Dakota, for the period ending 30 September 1960." Ellsworth Air Force Base, South Dakota, 54th Fighter Interceptor Squadron, declassified, November 20, 1978. Montgomery, Alabama: Maxwell Air Force Base, Air Force Historical Research Agency (Tammy T. Horton, CD/Microfilm Department) to author, June 16, 2015.

"History of atomic cloud sampling." Atomic Energy Commission Technical Library, SWEH-2-0034, dated January 1963, Air Force Weapons Library (declassified August 5, 1957).

"History of South Dakota Air and Space Museum." South Dakota Air and Space Museum, historical archives to author.

"History of the 54th Fighter Interceptor Squadron." Records retrieved by MSgt. Robert O'Daniel, Administrative Clerk after the squadron was discontinued to author.

"History of 54th Fighter-Interceptor Squadron." Ellsworth Air Force Base Public Affairs.

"Hughes AIM-4 Falcon." Dayton, Ohio: Wright Patterson Air Force Base, National Museum of the United State Air Force, "Cold War Gallery."

Information extracted from "Status of Work Items as of January 7, 1955." Prepared by the office in charge, Midwest Engineering District and Construction Office, US Army Corps of Engineers, Kansas City, Missouri.

Interview of members of the 3081st Aviation Group, Ellsworth Air Force Base, South Dakota. Lt. Col. George A. Larson, USAF (Ret.), August 14, 1995.

"Japanese Balloon display." Denver, Colorado: Colorado State Historical Society.

Lamb Associates, Inc. "Site Summary, Ellsworth Air Force Base (Rushmore Air Force Station), South Dakota." Albuquerque, New Mexico: Sandia National Laboratories, 1994.

Larson, George A., Major, USAF. "Review of the nation's air defense system and transitions during the Cold War." Material prepared for a research paper for the United States Air War College Non-resident Program." Updated in May 2015.

Larson, Lt. Col. George A. USAF (Ret.). *Thunder Over Dakota, The Complete History of Ellsworth Air Force Base*, South Dakota, Chapter Six, "Nike Ajax and Nike Hercules." Atglen, PA.: Schiffer Publishing, Ltd., 2013.

Letter from Headquarters Air Defense Command to Commander 54th Fighter-Interceptor Squadron, Ellsworth Air Force Base, South Dakota, dated November 1, 1957.

"Lockheed P-38 Lighting," specifications and performance information. Dayton, Ohio: Wright Patterson Air Force Base, National Museum of the United States Air Force, "World War II Gallery."

"McDonnell-Douglas AIR-2A Genie Rocket." Dayton, Ohio: Wright-Patterson Air Force Base, National Museum of the United States Air Force, "Cold War Gallery."

Mikesh, Robert C. *Japan's World War II Balloon Bomb Attacks on North America.* Washington, DC.: National Air and Space, Smithsonian Institution Press, 1973.

Morison, Samuel Elliot. *The Two Ocean War.* New York: Ballatine Books, 1963.

National Atomic Museum. "Today it is named," The National Museum of Nuclear Science and Technology. Albuquerque, New Mexico, National Atomic Museum Foundation.

The National Museum of Nuclear Science and Technology. "MB-1/Air-2 Genie Missile." Albuquerque, New Mexico, July 2009.

Neely, Harold L. Brig. Gen., USAF. Commander, Headquarters 29th Air Division (Defense) (ADC), United States Air Force, Malmstrom Air Force Base, Montana, "Commendation," to Commander, 54th Fighter- Interceptor-Squadron, Ellsworth Air Force Base, South Dakota, December 15, 1958.

"Nike-Ajax surface-to-air missile." Dayton, Ohio: Wright-Patterson Air Force Base, National Museum of the United States Air Force, "Cold War Gallery."

The Nike Historical Society. "Hercules MIM-14, MIM-14A, MIM-14B," (http://nikemissile.org/IFC/nike_hercules.shtml).

"Nike Missile Sites." Carlisle Barracks, Pennsylvania: United States Institute for Military History, United States Army War College.

"Nike Missile Sites at Ellsworth Air Force Base." Ellsworth Air Force Base, 28th Bomb Wing Historian.

"North American F-86D Sabre Dog," specifications and performance information. Dayton, Ohio: Wright Patterson Air Force Base, National Museum of the United States Air Force, "Cold War Gallery."

"North American P-51 Mustang," specifications and performance information. Dayton, Ohio: Wright Patterson Air Force Base, National Museum of the United States Air Force, "World War II Gallery."

"Northrop J-89J Scorpion," specifications and performance information. Dayton, Ohio: Wright Patterson Air Force Base, National Museum of the United States Air Force, "Cold War Gallery."

Nuckols, Commander, 54th Fighter-Interceptor Squadron, Ellsworth Air Force Base, South Dakota, November 1, 1960.

O'Daniel, MSgt. Robert. Rapid City, South Dakota, to author, May 15, 2012.

Ranney, Paul. Chairman, Military Affairs Committee, Rapid City Chamber of Commerce, to Lt. Col. Ernest D.

"Republic F-84E," specifications and performance information. Dayton, Ohio: Wright Patterson Air Force Base, National Museum of the United States Air Force, "Cold War Gallery."

"Rocket Training pays hit dividend to 54th." *Air Force Times*, Springfield, Virginia, March 17, 1956.

731st Radar Squadron. "A guide to Sundance Air Force Station Wyoming." Sundance, Wyoming: Marvin C. Hamilton, Major, USAF, Commander, 731st Radar Squadron, Air Defense Command, September 19, 1960.

United States Corps of Engineers, Chicago District. "Frontline of Defense, Nike Missile Sites in Illinois," Denver, Colorado: Department of Interior, National Park Service, Rocky Mountain Support Office, 1996.

"What is AMARG?" 309th Aerospace Maintenance and Regeneration Group, Administration to author June 12, 2015. Also available at (http://www/amarcexperience.com)

Yenne, Bill. *The History of the US Air Force*. New York: Bison Books, 1984.